Acknowledgments

To all those who contributed to the writing of this book through assistance, inspiration and encouragement, I express my thanks. Special thanks to my family: Jackie, Jonathan and Collin, who have patiently allowed me the evenings and days which otherwise could have been family time, and who shared experiences with three mission congregations in a fire station, a public school and a Holiday Inn.

I also thank the members of First Baptist Church, The Colony, Texas, and members of the Green Oaks Baptist Church of Arlington, Texas. They expanded my horizons regarding church planting and prayed for the completion of this book.

I must also thank Texas Baptist Woman's Missionary Union and their executive director, Joy Fenner, who saw the value of this book for missions, and the "Baptist Building family" in Texas: J.V. Thomas, my supervisor and the most creative, visionary Christian I have known; Dr. Charles Lee Williamson, director of missions division, for encouraging the publication of this manuscript from the beginning; Dr. Eugene Greer, program director for the state missions commission, for reading and re-reading the manuscript and offering suggestions; and the Church Extension staff of the Baptist General Convention of Texas.

Finally, I express my appreciation to Jack Redford and the staff of the Home Mission Board for making possible the publication and distribution of this book.

Table of Contents

A Tim

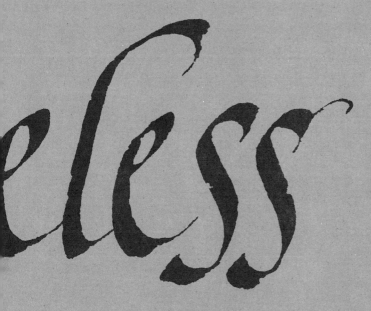

STRATEGY

Twenty centuries have passed since Jesus first gave his command, "Go therefore and make disciples of all the nations" (Matt. 28:19, NASB). More than 100 generations of Christians have run their life-races, passing from each to each this flaming mission mandate, yet the completion of the task still remains far from sight. Only 25 percent of the world's population professes the slightest assent to his Lordship, and half of the world's three billion people have never heard the name of Jesus Christ. The best projections indicate erosion of even this small impact on the world's population: only 16 percent will profess him as their savior as this century closes. Did Jesus intend to reach only a "reasonable percentage" of the world's population? Did Jesus intend that his command should be fulfilled or did he give his disciples an impossible imperative?

The author of the Great Commission provided the means for

his every command to be fulfilled. When he commanded the lame to walk, atrophied bone and sinew, muscle and nerve sprang to life (Luke 5:24)! When he commanded the deaf to hear, it was sound stimulus previously unknown to those silent senses (Mark 7:32-35)! When he commanded Peter to step from the boat, he provided firmness of foot on the watery wave (Matt. 14:29)!

In all the Scripture, Jesus never gave a command he did not intend to be fulfilled. And in all the Scripture, God provided the means by which the commanded could obey.

We can only conclude that Jesus both intended for this, his greatest command, to be obeyed—and provided the means for its fulfillment.

So why has the church fallen short? Where has the Christian movement gone wrong?

Each generation has marshaled new strategies and manufactured arsenals of spiritual resources to carry out Christ's command. With sword in hand, some have fielded whole armies, launched great armadas and led bloody crusades to Christianize the world.

Some have retreated into monastic solitude, fleeing temptation and forging fortresses of moral purity. Others have hoped to convert the world using mass circulation of the printed message. The 15th century advent of the printing press disseminated the written word to homes and factories. During the Reformation, God's Spirit moved all Europe on paper sails and rivers of ink.

Still others have looked to education as the strategy for fulfilling the Great Commission. Institutions of learning have been founded throughout the world so that young and old, rich and poor, might discover for themselves the Kingdom truth.

As the 20th century draws to a close, the strategies have taken an increasingly technological turn. Word processing, video and audio recording, computerization and satellite transmission have become household concepts to the Christian community. From strategy to strategy, generations have turned, each with its own measure of merit.

But what is the *one* strategy by which Christ's desire might be accomplished? His changeless strategy is found in the summary statement made to Peter, "Upon this rock I will build my church, and the gates of hell shall not prevail against it" (Matt. 16:18). This statement of Jesus, simple yet

*Upon this rock I will build my church, and the gates of hell shall not prevail against it."
(Matthew 16:18)*

profound, provides both a seedbed for understanding and a mooring to which the church must constantly return when examining the strategic actions necessitated by the Great Commission. Within this statement lie the dynamic, the design and the dimensions of his strategy.

The dynamic of his strategy

The dynamic of his strategy is divine, supernatural: "I will build My church." Often-times as much significance is found in what Jesus did not say as in what he did say. In this case, the significance lies in the fact that he did not say, "*Men* shall build the church." Neither did he say, "*You* shall build the church." In contrast, his statement is clearly in the first person, "*I* will build my church."

This dynamic is integral to the very nature of the church. It is no mere human institution that can be explained only in terms of sociology or philosophy. Any attempt to examine the church strategy in terms that ignore the supernatural is inadequate, approaching a multi-dimensional subject with a single dimensional vision. *Ignorance of the supernatural dynamic results in erroneous conclusions*.

The church has been infused with the creative agency of Christ from its beginning. He whose nature it is to initiate and create, says of the church, "I will build."

Without this supernatural dynamic, the church degenerates into a mere social institution with little to distinguish it from the United Way, Kiwanis, Lions Club or Boy Scouts of America. All are effective and needed institutions, but none claims a supernatural dynamic.

It is perhaps in this area that the world most frequently questions the church. Is there something in the church that cannot be found anywhere else? Is there a divine presence?

Quite clearly the church has made progress toward fulfillment of its purpose—to disciple all nations—only when this dynamic has been present. Of that initial expansion within the church at Jerusalem, much is attributed to the fact that "everyone kept feeling a sense of awe; and many wonders and signs were taking place through the apostles" (Acts 2:43, NASB). This sense of the spiritual dynamic at Jerusalem continued to be fueled by the healing of the lame beggar at the temple gate (Acts 3:6-8), the prayer meeting following the threat by Jewish authorities

(Acts 4:24-31), the sacrificial giving among the Christians (Acts 4:32-37), and the miraculous release of the apostles from prison (Acts 5:17-32). Without this sense of God's presence, growth of the church at Jerusalem would scarcely have occurred.

Even a cursory reading of the remainder of the book of Acts reveals the significance of this divine power in church planting at Antioch, Cyprus, Lystra, Philippi, Thessalonica, Athens, Corinth and Ephesus. Can churches be expected to grow in great numbers and to impact the lost world on any other grounds? Certainly not! But how *can* this take place?

First, Christians must recognize God's moving in the world, in the churches and in individual lives. Too often his activity goes unrecognized: it is dismissed as "men drunk with wine at the third hour of the day," or as some magically formulated program to lure the masses.

It is astounding that so many Jewish and Gentile leaders could ignore the intervention of God in their day, viewing the sacred events as commonplace, or as threats to the status quo. However, today's generation may unwittingly be guilty of the same. What has been called commonplace may be the activity of God; and what is viewed as a threat to the established organizations and traditions of churches may be evidence of his Spirit. Men must cultivate an eye for the divine dynamic that perceives another dimension.

Second, God must be depended upon to send an outpouring of his Spirit without measure. The true moving of the Spirit of God within his churches cannot be manufactured by programs and techniques. The significant moments of old when God intervened to alter the course of history were not moments fashioned by human hands. Moses did not seek nor anticipate the implications of turning aside to examine a bush burning upon the mountain (Exodus 3). Peter scarcely could have imagined the journey he was about to begin when accepting Andrew's invitation (John 1:40-42). Saul of Tarsus could not conceive the radical change awaiting his life as he set out for Damascus (Acts 9). Nor could Martin Luther have predicted the impact of his 95 theses.

When God moves dynamically in the lives of men, he will leap denominational lines and eclipse every strategy and program devised by man. Not every generation experi-

What has been called commonplace may be the activity of God; what is viewed as threat to established organizations and traditions may be evidence of his Spirit.

ences such a moving of God's Spirit. Let us pray that it happens in our lifetime.

The design of his strategy

The design of Christ's strategy is the church, the *ekklesia*: "I will build my *church*." The Apostles caught the expansion of the church as the pivotal cog through which the power of God would be transferred into the world.

To remove from the New Testament those things related to planting and growing congregations would delete virtually the volume of Scripture that emerged after Jesus Christ's Great Commission in Matthew 28. The book of Acts is largely devoted to events and circumstances of church planting in Asia Minor and Europe. The letters of the apostle Paul (Romans, 1 and 2 Corinthians, Galatians, Ephesians, Philippians, Colossians, 1 and 2 Thessalonians) are all occasioned by the planting of churches in these strategic cities. From them may be gleaned a wealth of material regarding doctrinal and practical foundations for new church growth. Add to the list the pastoral letters to Timothy and Titus, since they were converts from the church planting process and assistants to Paul in the nurture and expansion of congregations. Even the book of Revelation is addressed to the churches of Asia Minor, all of which were established by implementation of Christ's strategy.

To remove the strategy of church planting from the New Testament would in effect remove all Scripture beyond the gospels. The disciples and apostles made church planting their strategy to penetrate first century society!

Christ's strategy offered flexibility. He did not devote great portions of his teaching to ensure exact blueprints for the development of his church. As it grew, the church developed offices for leadership, instruction, administration and ministry, as well as music and liturgy. But Jesus did not see these aspects as definitive of his strategy. He avoided calcified organizational structures that could not adapt to changing cultures. Jesus refused to reduce his strategic design to brick and mortar.

The book of Acts and the Pauline letters demonstrate little concern for property purchase and building construction. Neither did the first century followers of Jesus focus

Jesus did not devote great portions of his teaching to ensure exact blueprints for development of his church. He refused to reduce his strategic design to brick and mortar.

upon buildings to define the presence of the *ekklesia*. Careful research of the Scriptures reveals only a blurred image of meeting facilities of the first century church—yet its ability to evangelize and affect life was awesome.

Perhaps this century suffers from an over-identification of the church with buildings that house it. Church buildings on corners of major thoroughfares offer a false sense of security. The land appears to be "churched," yet millions are untouched by the gospel and the *koinonia* of a church family. In Texas, a state at the "buckle of the Bible belt," more than seven million people are unrelated to any church. Gleaming white church spires rise above rooftops while cross-tipped shadows fall upon oblivious multitudes.

Even if all the church buildings were filled to capacity, the majority of Americans would be outside the walls of the church.

Jesus Christ's design is to create a people distinguished by their "called out" relationship to the Father. Without a new nature, followers produce organizations and structures doomed to the same corruption that grips the socio-political structures of the era. Yet as these people experience transformation, their varied structures, operations and organizations would be in-breathed with redemption.

His design is couched in terms of people: the *ekklesia* is a term for assembly. Its simple form is two-fold: people in relation to God, and people in relation to people.

People in relation to God

Ekklesia presupposes a "calling out." The term is a binding of two Greek terms, *kaleo*, meaning "to call" and the preposition *ek* meaning "out." It reflects the literal experience of people being called to assembly by a given signal, of trumpet, bells or human shouts. Christ's design is that love of God be supreme in the lives of those who are "called out." The difficulty arises in their loving God as he truly is.

Most men love God "made in their own image." To the degree that image is challenged, chipped or fractured, they may resist, even to the point of violence. The key is to love God so supremely that he shatters and shapes all of those preconceived images into a sharper image of himself.

The process of conforming to the image of God is painful, difficult and cause for feelings of insecurity. The book of Acts reveals a people whose God was coming into sharper focus and consequently shaping their lives. Yet the assumption that God could be known in a mere lifetime— let alone a few short decades—is the height of presumption. The character of his "called-out" people will not exhibit pompous boasting of ultimate knowledge of God, but humble submission in a supreme love of him that is open to new discovery of his person and presence.

People in relation to people

His design is also for a people to love one another as they love their very lives. Christ's focus upon this essential characteristic is unmistakable: "A new command I give you, that you love one another as I have loved you," and "By this shall all men know you are my disciples, that you have love one for another." Jesus did not conceive of his *ekklesia* existing apart from this love. Without love among the brethren, the church ceases to be. So great was the quality of love among the disciples that the church begins its expression with all members holding all things in common. Even the murmuring among members in Acts 6 is evidence that selfless care of one another was the expected expression of the church and that the lack of universal care for the entire fellowship was intolerable.

Paul eloquently penned his statements on love in 1 Corinthians 13. From this lofty vantage point, all other aspects of the church are placed in perspective. From this "height," he peered over the landscape of the church to proclaim, "If I speak with the tongues of men and angels, but do not have love, I have become a noisy gong, or a clanging cymbal. And if I have the gift of prophecy, and know all mysteries and all knowledge; and if I have all faith, so as to remove mountains, and have not love, I am nothing. And if I give all my possessions to feed the poor, and if I deliver my body to be burned, but do not have love, it profits me nothing." To this, virtually the entire letter of 1 John agrees.

The spirit of John called *Boanerges*, son of thunder, was transformed from prejudices and hate into a defender of this essential characteristic of the *ekklesia:* "The one who hates his brother is in the darkness . . . the one who loves his brother abides in the light . . . We know we have passed out of death into life because we love the brethren. He who

By this all men shall know you are my disciples, that you have love one for another." Jesus did not conceive of his ekklesia existing apart from this love.

does not love abides in death. Everyone who hates his brother is a murderer."

In too many instances, buildings have been constructed and persons have been organized without the essential element of *agape* love. As a result, the church has demonstrated its ability to develop budgets and fill calendars, but in the end it has produced only sounding brass and clanging cymbals. While churches may exist with a myriad of organizational structures expressing themselves in a variety of music and liturgy and occupying diverse accommodations, the church cannot exist without a sense of *agape* and koinonia among its members.

Yet Christ's design for the church is not just Christians in relation to Christians, but Christians in relation to non-Christians. If his design for the church were to turn totally inward, the church would smolder to ashes rather than ignite a flame of compassion and redemption transforming the hearts of men and women across vast planes of time and space. His imagery for the church is clearly one of aggressive redemption: "the gates of Hell shall not withstand its onslaught." Against all other devices, the gates of Satan's sanctuary remain unscathed, but against the irresistible force of the church, his gates shudder, giving way to the masterful advance of Christ's body in the world. Jesus created various metaphors dealing with the redemptive search of the church.

Characterizing his disciples as "salt" and "light" goes to the core of *ekklesia*. Though each of these elements has diverse individual characteristics, both are able to penetrate. Salt penetrates and permeates the substance in which it is placed; the smallest light penetrates and dispels the surrounding darkness.

To conceive of Christ's design for the *ekklesia* apart from evangelism is impossible. If the Son of Man came to seek and save that which was lost, so his body, the church, must be about the same task. The church finds its reason for being not in providing a sanctuary for those already saved, but in compassion, sacrifice and bold penetration of the darkness with the message of Jesus Christ that those who are lost may be saved.

People of weakness

That the design of Christ's strategy should be woven of

> *The church has demonstrated its ability to develop budgets and fill calendars, but in the end it has produced only sounding brass and clanging cymbals.*

human flesh presents a paradox. How can the ideals of ultimate love for God, sacrificial love for the brethren and redemptive love for the world be carried out by men and women who inherently fall short in their love of God, who are concerned more about self than others, and who feel inadequate and fearful of any bold attempts to carry the redemptive message to the world? It appears that the church is defeated before it has begun. It seems that Jesus failed to take into account the human obstacles that would doom his design to mere dreaming.

Yet those nearest Jesus were convinced that "he needed no man to tell him what was in the heart of man." To Peter he would say, "Get thee behind me, Satan, for you savour not the things that be of God, but the things of men." Having perceived weakness before it found expression, Jesus beheld Peter denying him thrice.

Certainly Jesus did not develop his design for the church with a blind eye to human frailty. In his own Gethsemane struggle, Jesus Christ acknowledged the willing spirit but weak flesh of the human condition.

The church in this world is composed of men and women who—like Lazarus from the tomb—bring with them decaying grave clothes that carry the stench of death. As a result, churches are composed of men and women who relate to one another at varying degrees of spiritual maturity and worldly carnality. At times the church rises to its zenith showing devotion, love and redemption. At other times it descends to the depths, expressing hostility, prejudice, envy and self-centeredness. Like those humans who compose its membership, the church has infinite capacity for the divine and the demonic.

This phenomenon is not isolated to the 20th century. A study of Paul's letters in the New Testament reveals that the early church also struggled with this paradox.

The first century church at Corinth was ensnared in jealousy and immorality. Paul did not hesitate to publicly confront the cliques forming around personalities; nor did he gloss over the slanderous relationship being tolerated within the church membership: one young man was living in sexual relationship with his father's wife. Neither did he fail to address the fact that fellow Christians were dragging one another into civil court over property disputes.

The church at Galatia had gone into a doctrinal tailspin,

At times the church rises to zenith, showing devotion, love and redemption. At other times it descends to depths, expressing hostility, prejudice, envy and self-centeredness.

9

"deserting him who called you by the grace of Christ, for a different gospel." Influenced by Judaizers, they had succumbed to the traditions of Judaism and built again a legalistic approach to salvation. Paul also indicated disharmony among the members when he wrote, "The whole Law is fulfilled in one word, in the statement, You shall love your neighbor as yourself. But if you bite and devour one another, take care lest you be consumed by one another."

Paul eloquently exhorted the Ephesians to put away the practices of their pre-Christian lives: sensuality, impurity and greed. Theft and falsehood were to be replaced with diligent labor and honesty. His exhortations reflect the tensions within the Christian community.

Perhaps this contrast between divine potential and human weakness existing in the churches is best demonstrated in Jesus Christ's statements to the seven churches of Asia Minor as recorded by John in the Revelation.

The Ephesians' remarkable perseverance and endurance was offset by departure from their first love.

Smyrna's spiritual wealth in the midst of physical poverty would be tested by arduous persecution.

Pergamum's commendable refusal to deny the faith while under Satanic pressure contrasted its toleration of the teaching of Balaam and the Nicolatians.

The church at Thyatira accomplished greater deeds than ever before, yet it was tolerating immorality.

Sardis enjoyed a great reputation among the churches and the world, but underneath its glamorous exterior was inner spiritual decay.

Philadelphia demonstrated little power, yet before it stretched almost endless potential.

Laodicea achieved "financial freedom"—demonstrating the economic power of the gospel—but was lured into lukewarm apathy, trusting in financial strength while becoming spiritually blind and poverty-stricken.

This paradox is sharpened by the limits of man's own mortality. Saintly men and women who as anointed spokespersons for God have seen horizons unknown to the rest, are silenced by the grave and replaced by younger, less experienced and less mature believers.

If God is to work in this generation to accomplish his purposes, he will work through weak flesh. Each generation must make itself available.

This is Christ's strategy. Churches, conceived with love for the Father, sacrificial love for the family and redemptive love for non-Christians, paradoxically are composed of human beings locked in a carnal struggle with imperfection: divine "treasure in earthen vessels."

The dimension of Christ's strategy

The supernatural dynamic and the simple design of Jesus Christ's nuclear statement are essential to the accomplishment of his task: "The gates of hell shall not prevail against it."

The church was conceived by Jesus because of the heavy gloom hanging over the human spirit and suffocating man's highest ambitions for integrity and peace. Sad, indeed, it is for men to live in a world of moral and spiritual darkness, where nightmarish phantoms of lust, greed and selfish indulgence are released without restraint. But sadder still is the human spirit that lives unaware of the darkness that engulfs it and without a yearning for a new light to dawn. It is to those who cry out in abhorrence of evil and lift their heads in pursuance of good, Jesus said, "Upon this rock I will build my church."

Jesus accurately perceived and portrayed the spiritual darkness in which this world is gripped. It is the darkness of death. His word for hell is hades, Sheol, the realm of the dead. Without Christ, without the cross, all humanity is under the sentence of death. Man is "condemned already" (John 3:18). "Death has passed upon all men because all have sinned" (Rom. 5:12).

In Christ, alone, is the hope of life. Peter's confession is discovery of this hope. And in the possession of the church are the keys of life and death as the gospel is proclaimed, and as men and women are discipled.

Quite apart from a creeping darkness that lengthens its shadows into a world of diminishing light, Jesus saw a world under a dark cloud of death. Into that darkness he introduced a light that threatens to lay bare the sinister and treacherous presence of the evil one.

Too often the church has been viewed as a sanctuary of retreat from an evil world. Too often Christians have hidden behind stained glass windows and with loud music have drowned out the cries of an anguished world.

It is Satan's stronghold which is threatened. The

Too often Christians have hidden behind stained glass windows and with loud music have drowned out the cries of an anguished world.

11

foundations of his doomed kingdom quake at the advance of the church. His citadel is under siege.

The dimension of Jesus Christ's strategy includes every strata of society from those with political power to the poor and weak. The church alone is uniquely equipped to penetrate every segment of humanity.

Questions for pastors and churches:

1. Is our church experiencing the dynamic presence of God? Is there a sense of the supernatural in our church?

2. Is our church committed to the realization of the Great Commission, or are we content with a "reasonable percentage"?

3. What is the key strategy envisioned by Jesus and practiced by the apostles in order to realize the Great Commission?

4. Am I allowing God to shape my image of him or am I clinging to preconceived ideas of his reality?

5. Are Christian *agape* and *koinonia* evident in our church?

6. Does our church evidence the paradox of spiritual maturity and worldly carnality?

7. What are positive attributes of our church that will enable it to achieve its potential?

8. What obstacles would hinder our church from fulfilling its potential?

9. Is our church in a defensive position, trying to hold its own against a world of darkness; or is it in an offensive position, penetrating the darkness with the message of light?

hrist's strategy includes every strata of society from those with political power to the poor and weak. The church is uniquely equipped to penetrate every segment.

13

THE
Multip

lication

DIMENSION

The world functions on the basis of multiplication. Multiplication is the arithmetic function of the 20th and 21st centuries, evident in population growth, technological expansion and financial investment.

Observers of world population trends tremble at the portent of the future as the number of human beings continues to multiply, taxing resources for food, housing and employment, and reducing chances for peace.

The technological revolution continues, its exponential growth unabated as daily innovations prove obsolete within months, if not days. With the mushrooming technological market, investors in computer hardware and software are shocked to find recent investments outmoded.

Multi-million dollar empires continue to be built by those who know well how to multiply their investments.

More and more, the difference between understanding and confusion, between success and defeat, between survival and death, is the difference between multiplication and addition.

Adding disciples in a multiplying world

Here lies a salient problem of the church: it is employing the wrong arithmetic function. It is attempting to penetrate a world of multiplication with simple addition.

Here lies a salient problem of the church: it is employing the wrong arithmetic function. It is attempting to penetrate a world of multiplication with simple addition.

Each year, churches are *adding* new converts to the kingdom. They will baptize approximately the same number of persons baptized the year before. In other denominations, this growth principle is the same.

The D. James Kennedy program of Evangelism Explosion (which has built into its design the multiplication factor by having one person train two, and each train two others and so on) soon breaks down into mere addition within the local church. A single congregation will assimilate only so many new converts. Evangelism Explosion International has quickly recognized that multiplication of disciples only takes place as multiplied numbers of churches adopt this plan of discipling and witness. Consequently their strategy has moved to developing regional clinics for new church enlistment.

Even such super churches as First Baptist, Dallas, or North Phoenix Baptist Church in Arizona, are limited to growth by addition. Although they may each baptize 300, 400 or 500 persons in one year, these churches will baptize about the same number the next year. If average attendance increases by 200 in one year, it will not likely increase by much more than 200 in the year to follow.

This principle holds true for churches of any size. Each church baptizes approximately the same number it baptized the year before, and most churches average approximately the same attendance averaged the year before.

With the churches which exist today, growth will consist of addition, at best. With this in mind, John Bisagno, pastor of the rapidly growing First Baptist, Houston, is leading his church to sponsor 20 new congregations in the next 10 years.

In the context of the entire Christian movement, the church is structured for a ministry of addition rather than a ministry of multiplication.

Existing churches simply could not build fast enough, nor adequately expand their organizations, leadership and assimilation structures to disciple an exponential growth of new converts. The church planning for multiplied disciples must plan for multiplied churches.

The secret of multiplying disciples

Texas Baptists recently completed a study relative to church age and attendance. Tracking attendance through annual reports submitted by Southern Baptist churches in Texas, and categorizing these by the age of each church, the graph in Table 1 was produced.

For churches five years of age, attendance averaged 145. Churches more than 100 years old averaged 155. As noted in the graph, churches between these ages averaged more or less the same. This does not mean that some churches will not grow well beyond 150 average attendance. Some will reach well over 1,000. But these are balanced by a greater number of churches which never reach 100 in average attendance.

Churches as a group reach their potential for growth within the first five years of existence. While some will continue to grow for many years, and while others will experience new growth after years of plateaued or even declining conditions, most will remain relatively small. This is not a value judgment. It is an observable fact. As a whole, Texas churches affiliated with the Southern Baptist Convention average 145 to 155—regardless of age—after the fifth year of existence.

Given this reality, the following conclusions may be drawn:

(1) The continued addition of new disciples likely will not exceed the number of members exiting the church through dropout, transfer and death.

(2) Given the current number of churches, the multiplication of disciples is highly unlikely and more probably, impossible.

(3) Significant addition of disciples will necessitate significant addition of churches.

(4) The multiplication of disciples will require multiplication of churches.

(5) The multiplication of churches will produce multiplied disciples.

Churches as a group reach their potential for growth within the first five years of existence. Most will remain relatively small.

Table 1

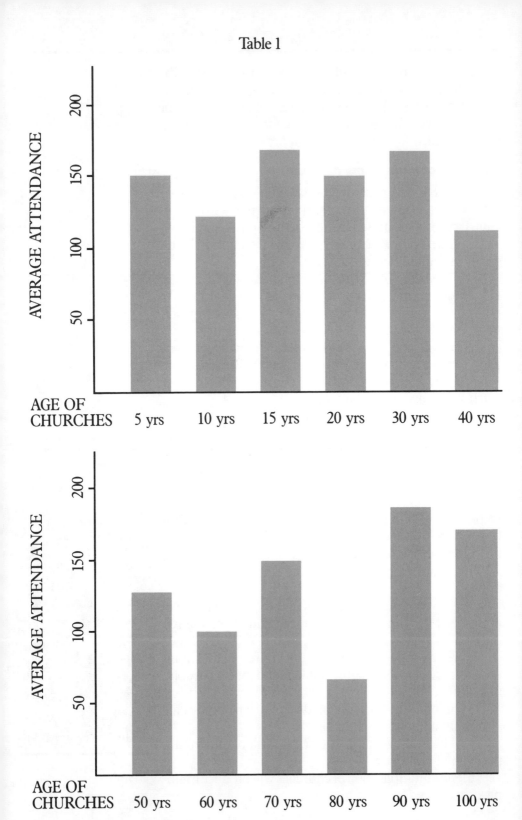

Table 2

CHANGE IN NUMBER OF SBC CHURCHES
BY STATE CONVENTION, 1970-1982

State Convention	Churches 1970	Source of Church Change				Churches 1982	Change 1970-1982	
		Added	Re-organized	Dropped	Net Transfers		Number	Percent
Alabama	2,932	215	29	151	0	3,025	93	3.2%
Alaska	36	11	1	5	0	43	7	19.4
Arizona	225	63	1	37	-16	236	11	4.9
Arkansas	1,190	128	10	63	-1	1,264	74	6.2
California	861	287	9	134	-28	995	134	15.6
Colorado	122	77	3	30	0	172	50	41.0
DC	60	6	1	5	-5	57	-3	-5.0
Florida	1,448	265	12	140	1	1,586	138	9.5
Georgia	2,968	242	29	257	0	2,982	14	0.5
Hawaii	31	9	0	2	0	38	7	22.6
Illinois	901	126	5	123	1	910	9	1.0
Indiana	226	102	1	51	2	280	54	23.9
Kans.-Neb.	200	55	3	30	-1	227	27	13.5
Kentucky	2,194	150	42	161	-8	2,217	23	1.1
Louisiana	1,309	77	16	77	0	1,325	16	1.2
Maryland	278	83	3	24	-28	312	34	12.2
Michigan	168	74	5	53	0	194	26	15.5
Mississippi	1,883	129	18	94	2	1,938	55	2.9
Missouri	1,825	201	13	151	-1	1,887	62	3.4
Nevada	0	12	1	2	44	55	55	NA
New Mexico	244	39	3	25	0	261	17	7.0
New York	74	89	0	12	0	151	77	104.1
No. Carolina	3,449	237	18	220	0	3,484	35	1.0
No. Plains	79	98	3	17	3	166	87	110.1
Northwest	222	102	2	37	0	289	67	30.2
Ohio	402	184	9	81	-39	475	73	18.2
Oklahoma	1,368	152	14	91	1	1,444	76	5.6
Penn.-So. Jersey	0	63	0	12	48	99	99	NA
Puerto Rico	0	27	0	2	0	25	25	NA
So. Carolina	1,599	154	7	53	0	1,707	108	6.8
Tennessee	2,698	242	24	179	-1	2,784	86	3.2
Texas	3,870	576	35	423	-1	4,057	187	4.8
Utah-Idaho	64	29	1	9	-1	84	20	31.3
Virginia	1,434	102	10	74	-24	1,448	14	1.0
W. Virginia	0	36	0	3	52	85	85	NA
Total SBC	34,360	4,442	328	2,828	0	36,302	1,942	5.7%

Source: Uniform Church Letters and Research Department, Sunday School Board, Nashville, Tennessee

Possibly churches have lacked an effective growth strategy. While churches have been able only to add rather than multiply new converts, the denominations, conventions and associations have been able only to add churches.

Table 2 is the Home Mission Board report of new Southern Baptist churches added during the past decade. As will be easily noted, nowhere does there exist a multiplication of churches.

Current church starting may be contrasted with that of the first century. While Acts traced church planting efforts of Paul, the multiplication of churches was taking place in many other regions.

The church at Rome existed before Paul arrived. Peter recognizes the existence of churches at "Pontus, Galatia, Cappadocia, Asia and Bithynia" (1 Pet. 1:1). While the Holy Spirit prevented Paul from entering Asia and Bithynia (Acts 16:6-7), others successfully planted churches in these regions.

Church historians also verify that the real strength of the Christian movement by the second century was not in Europe but in North Africa where the first center for Christian thought was established at Alexandria by Pantaenus. The churches were multiplying geographically throughout the Mediterranean world. Simple addition could not have produced this level of penetration in only three centuries.

At the same time the church was multiplying in great regions, congregations were multiplying in communities. In Jerusalem alone, some estimate 1,500 congregations were meeting in homes.

In his epistles, Paul refers repeatedly to churches meeting in houses and homes:

"The churches of Asia greet you. Aquila and Prisca greet you heartily in the Lord, with the church that is in their house" (1 Cor. 16:19, NASB).

"Greet the brethren who are in Laodicea and also Nympha and the church that is in her house" (Col. 4:15).

"Greet Prisca and Aquila my helpers in Christ Jesus . . . Likewise greet the church that is in their house . . . Greet those who are of the household of Aristobulus . . . Greet those who are of the household of Narcissus" (Rom. 16: 3-11, NASB).

Three questions

Three questions must be asked concerning the "multiplication dimension": (1) Should churches multiply? (2) Can churches be multiplied? (3) How could churches be multiplied?

The first question is pivotal. Some feel that America is already churched, perhaps overchurched. This assumption is usually held by those who believe that established churches adequately provide worship opportunities for those who choose to worship, that there are plenty of churches "within driving distance."

This assumes a responsive mode on the part of the church: "Let those who would come, come." It ignores the aggressive position for the church as outlined by Christ. It fails to implement his injunction to go into the highways and byways and compel people to come in.

This thinking also assumes that buildings which are not full of people are evidence of the church with capacity for growth. Ironically, availability of space may be evidence that the the church is complete in terms of organizational structure and its ability to assimilate more people. On the other hand, the church which is full to overflowing with people may yet have capacity for assimilation, for growth.

A community populated with churches not filled to capacity may actually need additional churches to reach additional people.

On the basis of the philosophical foundation of the church and on the basis of practical opportunities for discipling people, it may be concluded that churches should multiply.

The second question is: could the church multiply? One answer is derived in retrospect. Certainly the church multiplied in the first century. But other periods have also produced church multiplication. Under the influence of Martin Luther, Ulrich Zwingli and John Calvin, the Reformation produced a veritable explosion of new churches. During this same period, severe persecution by both Catholics and Protestants could not stop a proliferation of Anabaptist churches. The Great Awakening of the 18th century swept across England and the American colonies, leaving in its wake thousands of new congregations of believers.

The churches were multiplying geographically throughout the Mediterranean world. Simple addition could not have produced this penetration in only three centuries.

*I*romically, availability of space may be evidence that the church is complete in terms of organizational structure and its ability to assimilate more people.

This second question must also be addressed. In mushrooming metropolitan regions with soaring land and building costs, in communities of diverse ethnicities and cultural values: can the church multiply once again?

Contemporary factors present not only the imperative but the climate.

Mushrooming metropolitan regions dictate the need for more churches. As thousands move to metropolitan centers, congregations must multiply. Many of these must be ethnic congregations to church the rapidly growing ethnic populations. Each ethnic group will require churches to serve persons of its various socio-economic segments.

Some churches will be housed in facilities vacated by dwindling Anglo populations in the inner city. Others will be housed in storefronts, houses, apartments and condominiums.

At the same time suburban churches must multiply to church the shifting and growing populations on the metropolitan fringe.

Escalation in cost of land and construction may necessitate greater risk in terms of land speculation in order to secure church sites. In other instances, more creative use of space may be required through the lease of shopping centers, houses, apartments, offices and club rooms. In some cases, churches may enter long-term lease contracts without permanent facilities. Real estate costs may encourage multiplication of smaller congregations less visible but more penetrating than the traditional church with steeple and stained glass.

These economic factors may actually give rise to the rapid proliferation of churches if this generation is indefatigably committed to the churching of society and fulfillment of the Great Commission.

Perhaps the most challenging question is the third: "How can churches multiply?" To address this question and all its ramifications reaches far beyond the scope or intent of this book. Yet some word must be said concerning the principles by which churches would multiply.

The begetting process

To multiply, churches must use the age-old process of begetting. It is one of the most powerful forces at work in the world. A man and woman beget their offspring. These beget children as well. My own family is an example. My parents had three sons. Although my older brother and his wife had no children, my wife and I had two sons; my younger brother and his wife had two sons and a daughter. All of this has resulted in a biological multiplication factor of more than two. Whereas only two persons occupied this planet four decades earlier, nine occupy it today. It would be difficult to orchestrate this growth from one organizational center. In the same way, periods of multiplied churches and disciples have most often taken place with a minimum of denominational directive.

Mission churches need mothers

Just as it would be hard to conceive of test tube babies populating the world, it would be difficult to conceive of redeeming the world with only centrally planned, clinically pure test tube congregations spun out of denominational laboratories. Churches must catch a vision of their own potential for begetting, while denominations serve obstetric and pediatric functions. This kind of denominational support will help insure healthy church growth and acceleration of church multiplication.

In the past, churches have relegated the starting of new churches to their denominational headquarters. But this is not enough. For example, of Southern Baptist churches in Texas, less than one church in 100 is giving birth to one new congregation each year.

An example of the multiplication factor unleashed through the birth of new congregations is found in the First Baptist Church of Lewisville, Texas. In the 1960s, when this church was averaging approximately 200, it sponsored Lakeland Baptist Church in that city. First Baptist continued to add disciples and Lakeland began adding disciples as well. In the early 1970s, First Baptist sponsored another mission, Orchard Road Baptist Church. In 1975, when First Baptist was averaging 320 in attendance, it sponsored the First Baptist Church, The Colony, a community approximately eight miles away. By this time *four* congregations were adding disciples. Subsequently the Lakeland Baptist Church, which had grown as strong as its mother, sponsored First Baptist Church of Highland Village, Farmersfield Baptist Church, West Side Baptist

Table 3

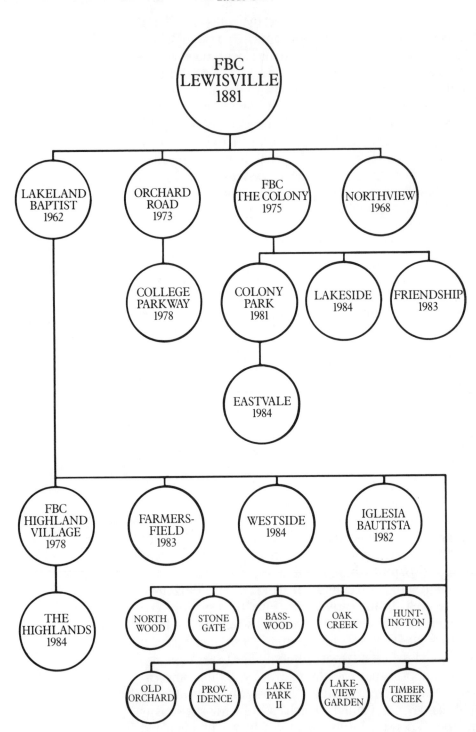

Church (Black congregation), Iglesia Bautista Lakeland (Hispanic), and 10 Indigenous Satellite Units (ISUs) in mobile home parks and apartment complexes. First Baptist, The Colony, gave birth to Colony Park Baptist, Friendship Baptist (Black), and now Lakeside Baptist Church. First Baptist Highland Village gave birth to the first "great-granddaughter" congregation when it sponsored The Highlands Baptist Church. Colony Park gave birth to the second when it sponsored the Eastvale Baptist Church. In 1985, First Baptist of Lewisville began yet another daughter church at High Meadows, just north of the city. In a space of 20 years, without being overly aggressive, the mission program of First Baptist Lewisville has resulted in 13 churches and 10 ISUs, all of which are adding disciples. A church which 20 years ago averaged 200 in attendance has given birth to congregations totaling almost 3,000 in attendance on a given Sunday. Table 3 charts multiplied church growth from First Baptist of Lewisville.

The measure of church "success" may need reevaluation. One day, a church may evaluate its fulfillment of Christ's commission not only on the basis of its attendance, its strength of fellowship, budget and cash flow, but by the number of congregations it begets.

Again, the "bride of Christ" can learn from the marriage institution. While marriage originated in the mind of God for human fellowship, that Adam might know one who was bone of his bone and flesh of his flesh, it was also instituted for procreation. Prior to the Fall, God issued his directive: "Be fruitful and multiply." If marriage were to result in greater fellowship between husband and wife, in greater emotional and financial security, but never in procreation, the human race would vanish from this planet.

The church fulfills its nature as the bride of Christ as it produces greater quality of spiritual and emotional life among its members and as it is fruitful and multiplies. A church can be the mother of many missions by sponsoring, simultaneously, numerous congregations. These new congregations, in turn, can sponsor others, so that given the extended life expectancy of a church, a multiplication factor greater than that of the population could be unleashed. In this event, the Great Commission could be fulfilled in this generation!

To multiply, churches must use the age-old process of begetting. It is one of the most powerful forces at work in the world.

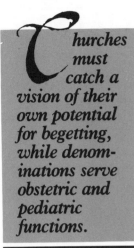

Churches must catch a vision of their own potential for begetting, while denominations serve obstetric and pediatric functions.

Questions for pastors and churches:

1. What church gave birth to our congregation? When?

2. How old is our church?

3. How does our average attendance today compare with the average attendance of our church 10 years ago?

4. How many people are added to our church each year?

5. Is our church growing by addition or by multiplication?

6. What is the population of our community?

7. How does the population of our community today compare with the population 10 years ago?

8. How could our church move from mere addition of disciples to multiplication of disciples?

9. How many daughter congregations has our church begotten in the last 10 years?

10. How many daughter congregations could our church beget in the next 10 years?

11. Could our church be the parent church of another congregation this year?

The measure of church "success" may need reevaluation. One day, a church may evaluate its fulfillment of Christ's commission by the number of congregations it begets.

THE

Et

DIMENSION

Nowhere is Jesus Christ's desire concerning the nations more evident than in his Great Commission: "Go therefore and make disciples of all the nations" (Matt. 28:19, NASB). In his statement, Jesus selects a precise word for the term "nations." It is literally the word ethne, the root of the English term "ethnic." Why did he not say, make disciples of "all men" (anthropoi), or "all mankind" or "of the world" (kosmos)? Why did he choose ethne?"

The Old Testament

This is no shift in the expressed redemptive purpose of God. From the beginning, his plan to redeem humanity was couched in ethnic terms. God's call to Abram to leave Haran and journey southward was a call with an intention: "In you all the families of the earth shall be blessed."

The prophets recognized this truth and called Israel to respond to redemptive responsibilities beyond its borders.

The Psalmist wrote, "I will praise thee, O Lord, among the people: and I will sing praises unto thee among the nations." Isaiah wrote, "Behold, thou shalt call a nation that thou knowest not, and nations that knew not thee shall run unto thee because of the Lord thy God, and for the Holy One of Israel, for he hath glorified thee." Daniel said: "And there was given him dominion, and glory, and a kingdom, that all people, nations, and languages, should serve him: his dominion is an everlasting dominion, which shall not pass away, and his kingdom that which shall not be destroyed." The prophet Micah concluded, "And many nations shall come, and say, Come, and let us go up to the mountain of the Lord, and to the house of the God of Jacob; and he will teach us of his ways, and we will walk in his paths: for the law shall go forth of Zion, and the word of the Lord from Jerusalem."

The agreement of the Old Testament prophets' words and the Great Commission of Christ is not incidental or accidental.

The ministry of Jesus

God's desire to frame his redemptive strategy in terms of the nations is evident in the life of Jesus. He is constantly aware of the ethnic and cultural issues which shape individual perceptions of the kingdom message. He infuriates the citizens of Nazareth, his home town, by reminding them that God sent Elijah to a Sidonian widow and Elisha to a leprous Syrian nobleman—while in Israel, countless widows and lepers remained in poverty and disease. With sensitivity to the ethnic implications of his healing a Syro-Phoenician woman's daughter, Jesus said, "I was sent only to the lost sheep of Israel." He astounds his disciples by not only traveling through the region of Samaria, but departing from his schedule to remain for two days near Sychar where he preached the message of life to those whom the Jews considered racially, culturally and spiritually inferior. Jesus did not hesitate to surface cultural differences which would hinder the reception of the truth or restrain its dissemination. He carefully refused to let the good news become identified with any one cultural expression, be it Jewish or Gentile. At the same time, he did not hesitate to

He carefully refused to let the good news become identified with any one cultural expression. At the same time, he did not hesitate to plant the gospel in any culture.

plant the gospel in any culture, thereby allowing the regenerate life to find variety of expression. The Galileans, Judeans, Samarians, Syro-Phoenecians and Gadarenes would have hardly expressed their faith in identical ways. Their languages and dialects as well as regional and national traditions varied greatly.

Could it be concluded that God foresaw and determined the redemption of men within the ethnic structures of the world?

The early church

Such a conclusion is reinforced by the experience unfolding in the first century church as recorded in Acts. The "paraclete" continues to move the church beyond its ethnic boundaries of culture and language.

The Pentecost experience itself swaddles the newly born ekklesia in the multi-colored cloth of the ethne: "Parthians and Medes and Elamites and residents of Mesopotamia, Judea and Cappadocia, Pontus and Asia, Phrygia and Pamphylia, Egypt and the districts of Libya around Cyrene, and visitors from Rome, both Jews and proselytes, Cretans and Arabs."

From the moment of its birth, the church continues to struggle with its task to disciple people of all cultural and linguistic groups of the world.

Even in this spiritually empowered beginning, the newly forming body of Christ has difficulty envisioning its expression outside a mono-cultural faith. Converts of the ethne are "God-fearers," proselytes of other nations who accepted Judaic traditions and teachings. The apostles do not conceive of "church" apart from Judaism. Yet they are soon faced with the possibility of new believers expressing their worship and lifestyle outside first century Judaism!

Peter's Caesarean experience sends shock waves through the Christian community. His conclusion that circumcision is not essential for belief and acceptance into the family of God is not only theologically but also practically significant. So significant is his housetop vision teaching him that nothing God has made is unclean, along with the subsequent conversion of Cornelius and his household, that this incident is recorded three times in Acts: first as it happened, second as initially reported by Peter, and finally as "exhibit A" at the Jerusalem council.

From the moment of its birth, the church continues to struggle with its task to disciple people of all cultural and linguistic groups of the world.

This incident above all else moves the first century church to abandon circumcision as a requirement for Christian discipleship. The theological implications of this decision, that salvation should be by faith in Christ alone, has already been explored. But the practical implications, both for the first century and for today, are often overlooked. The rite of circumcision was the strongest expression of cultural identity among the Jews. It was the link with Abraham, Isaac and Jacob. But the first century mission expeditions of Paul and Barnabas, added to the experience of Peter, forced the church to re-examine its stance. Would the Christian faith be disseminated only among groups which could identify with the Jewish culture and heritage, or would it be planted in all cultural contexts? The first century church chose the latter.

The preaching of Paul

The cultural variety finding expression throughout first century churches is evident in Paul's preaching and writing. In synagogues he preached of the exodus, the anointing of Saul, the greatness of David and the messianic prophecy of Christ. At Lystra he preached about the God of creation who called men from polytheistic worship to the living faith. At Athens he preached of the unknown god, creator of the cosmos and all humanity; and he called all to repentance and faith. His preaching always centered on the redemptive event of Christ. But his approach was determined by cultural perceptions.

In his letter to the Galatians, Paul clearly explained the theological implications of the Jerusalem Council decision regarding circumcision. He goes a step further by dropping the instruction to abstain from meat offered to idols. That this was a pointless issue in cultures outside Judaism surfaces in Paul's letter to the Romans. He establishes practical principles which foster respect for various cultural expressions of the Christian faith.

In response to issues related to consumption of meat offered to idols, the observation of holy days and special vegetarian or meat diets, Paul writes: "Let us not therefore judge one another any more: but judge this rather, that no man put a stumbling block or an occasion to fall in his brother's way. I know, and am persuaded by the Lord Jesus, that there is nothing unclean of itself: but to him that esteemeth anything to be unclean, to him it is unclean" (Romans 14). Paul's "persuasion of the Lord" is a persuasion not to identify the Christian faith with any particular cultural dimension. This conviction is set in bold relief against the pre-conversion convictions of Paul, the "Pharisee of the Pharisees."

The modern church and ethnicity

The dilemma of the early church, finding expression in different issues, continues today. Like a 20th century rocket exerting thousands of pounds of thrust to break away from the earth's gravitational pull, the church must make a concerted effort to free itself from the drag of cultural forces. Unattended, the church is drawn into cultural orbit. It assumes its cultural values are identical with the Christian message.

The gospel does not require people of every race and socio-economic stratum to worship in the manner of "our" church, dress as "we" dress, think as "we" think, speak as "we" speak. The gospel of Jesus Christ must transcend culture to reach all people.

A church may be able to reach people from distinctly different cultures and lifestyles as they are assimilated into the dominant culture. For instance, some Hispanics, Chinese, Koreans and others will feel more comfortable with Anglo worship and Bible study. Others will be reached only by their specific language congregations. Within each cultural group exist several cultural sub-groups with their individual expressions and worship.

A recent immigrant—such as the undocumented Hispanic person—might feel confused or ill at ease in an English-speaking congregation. This person would probably prefer to worship among those who speak his language and adhere to common cultural values. A bi-lingual Hispanic person who is a naturalized citizen or an American by birth may actually prefer to worship in an Anglo church. Or this same person may choose to worship with a sub-group of Hispanics who congregate according to common socio-economic or educational backgrounds.

Each congregation, singly, will be able to penetrate a clearly defined, cultural sub-group. And out of that sub-group, each congregation will be able to assimilate a relatively small percentage of the whole. The ethnic dimen-

The gospel does not require people of every race and socio-economic stratum to worship in the manner of our church, dress as we dress, think as we think, speak as we speak.

sion of Jesus Christ's strategy demands penetration of each of these sub-groups with a multitude of congregations. This means churches must develop a new eye for missions. For too long the church has looked at the mission field around it and seen men "as trees, walking." A second touch of the Physician's hand is needed that men may be seen clearly.

The ethnic dimension and ethical questions

This practical approach to missions gives rise to disturbing questions. How can the church commit itself to cultural strategies given the Christian mandate for unity among men and believers? Does the practical approach to ethnic and socio-economic missions yield division and prejudice? After the long struggle to achieve integration, does this strategy turn from the sunrise of racial unity toward the dark caverns of isolation and mistrust? These questions cannot hide behind the cloak of pragmatism. The concern for the church is not simply "What works?" but "What is right and true?" The following insights may prove helpful in the struggle over this difficult issue.

Adjectives and nouns

It is helpful to understand the differing cultural and racial distinctives as adjectives rather than nouns.

An individual should be perceived as a unique person, not a stereotype. The Laotian person is not merely "Laotian." The non-professional worker should be seen as an individual and not merely as "blue collar."

The Apostle's most definitive statement on this matter is found in Galatians: "There is neither Jew nor Greek, there is neither slave nor free man, there is neither male nor female; for you are all one in Christ Jesus" (Gal. 3:28). With this sweeping statement, the Scripture dissolves all distinction of those from a certain racial or cultural group as being different in terms of worth and value. Subsequently, the only noun left is that of person. All are one in Christ Jesus regardless of racial or cultural identity. At the same time, the Bible does not dismiss the distinctive uniqueness of racial and cultural groups, preserving these as adjectives.

There are different characteristics between Jew and Gentile, male and female, and in Paul's day, bond and free. The Apostle recognizes these differences in his statement to the Corinthians: "To the Jews I became as a Jew that I might win the Jews: to those who are under the Law, as under the Law . . . to those who are without the law, as without law . . . To the weak I became weak that I might win the weak; I have become all things to all men that I may by all means win some" (1 Cor. 9:20-22, NASB).

The Apostle recognized that the various cultural groups of his day would only be reached if the strategy for churching them took into account these differences. The call of the gospel is a call to recognize the universal worth and dignity of all men, not a call to bury heads in the sand and pretend no differences exist.

New wine in old wineskins

It is helpful to understand the ethnic dimension of the church in terms of Jesus Christ's parable regarding new wine in old wineskins. His reference to the inability of old and brittle wineskins to hold the swelling pressure of new wine is stimulated by his confrontation with the traditional and cultural structures of Judaism. His reference is clearly not to the law of God, for this law he embodied and fulfilled. Rather, he referred to a rigid culture that could not contain the universal ramifications of the gospel. The society of humankind is littered with old wineskins, with the cultural and traditional structures which separate races, nationalities and neighborhoods. Every attempt to destroy the wineskins from without results in rage, revolt and deeper hostilities between men.

When "wineskin" structures break during open conflict, they give rise to new traditions and cultures but often harbor a multitude of sub-cultures. The semblance of unity may be maintained with the ability of the dominant culture to control education, language, economics and the media.

The bursting of old wineskins is best done from within.

The unconverted Peter could hardly have envisioned himself in a Gentile home, let alone eating with Gentiles or defending their rights before his peers at Jerusalem. But the new wine of the gospel brought pressures from within that burst his earlier prejudices.

Perhaps even more dramatic is the account of Saul of Tarsus. This devoted Pharisee could scarcely conceive of a day when he would travel throughout the Gentile world promoting the inclusion of non-Jews into the messianic promise. But the brittle Pharisaic prejudices of his youth

35

could not contain the wine of the new life.

Recently a multi-ethnic group gathered at a Vietnamese restaurant for dinner: six were Laotians, one Cambodian, one American Indian and two Anglos. The new wine of Christ had broken the old wineskin barriers which once would have separated their spiritual, intellectual and emotional lives. Even language difficulties seemed incidental under the love of Jesus Christ, which does not demand the dissolution of culture but fully respects tradition and personhood.

Christ, not culture, becomes the link, the common ground. In him, children of differing cultures become "family."

Church buildings once filled with scrubbed white faces and echoing English hymns of praise are now home to a people of myriad expressions and race: red, yellow, brown and black. Churches are discovering ways to share facilities among various congregations, each with its distinctive cultural expression.

All discrimination and prejudice toward different groups should be unequivocally opposed by the Christian faith. This does not mean eradication of cultural and racial distinctives. And perhaps it is here that the world most flagrantly errs in its attempt to achieve racial equality. The dominant racial and cultural group, attempting to express humanitarian concern, may assume that persons must become like "us" to possess equal worth and value. Attempts at forced integration, etc., may become attempts to anglicize or caucasianize a subordinate group.

The Christian way affirms the worth and value of each person and defends, even promotes, the right to maintain cultural and racial distinctives. To the world these distinctives pose a constant threat to stability and harmony, for old wineskins cannot contain new wine.

Anglo churches in America too often have made the assumption that conversion and Christian discipleship lead to inevitable conclusions expressed in the Anglo culture. It is here, again, that Christians must exercise the inner discipline to divest themselves of one cultural identification and allow the gospel to find its idiomatic expression in the various cultures in which it is planted.

The cause is not eradication of meaningful adjectives that preserve differences of culture; the cause is the re-

> *The love of Jesus Christ does not demand the dissolution of culture but fully respects tradition and personhood. Christ, not culture, becomes the link, the common ground.*

demption of persons through the gospel of Jesus Christ.

The third consideration involves the greatness of God. The vast and rich personality of God demands that he be worshiped in a variety of languages and cultures. He is too great to be praised in one tongue, by one nation, one culture. If all peoples were integrated into one church, adopting one culture and one language, that would diminish the variety of praise of which he alone is worthy.

John's Revelation was of worship in which "they sang a new song saying, 'Worthy are Thou to take the book, and to break the seals; for Thou wast slain, and didst purchase for God with thy blood men from every tribe and tongue and people and nation'" (Rev. 5:9).

One final observation: while people will continue to group themselves around socio-economic, cultural and ethnic similarities, these conditions do not constitute the foundations of the church. They may describe expressions that the church will take in this world of diversity, but they are not a foundation other than that which has been laid.

The one foundation is Jesus Christ. We must never be lulled into the misconception that creating a gathering of people around similarities of income, preference, language, culture and condition constitutes a church. Nor does a gathering of people for other reasons—mutual benefit, shared causes, common interests—define the ekklesia. A church has been born only when individual lives are founded upon a living faith in Jesus Christ, and when that common faith binds those people together for discipling. "For no man can lay a foundation other than the one which is laid, which is Jesus Christ."

Questions for pastors and churches

1. Is our church open to receiving persons of all races?
2. Do we have members from various ethnic groups?
3. Is our community multi-ethnic?
4. Due to culture or language, would certain people feel uncomfortable in our church?
5. Could our church sponsor congregations of various ethnic groups in our community?
6. Does our church have space it could make available for an ethnic congregation?
7. Is our church and its mission truly founded upon the person of Jesus Christ?

37

THE

Netw

rking

DIMENSION

Networks refer to those dynamics by which people relate to people. Networks are the frequently traveled communication links that make life workable, meaningful and enjoyable. Networks are established along lines of common interest, mutual support and essential communication for performance of tasks. Consequently, people will build their networks through family, occupation and recreation.

In some cases network development will relate closely to geography. In other cases, it will not. The simple geographic grouping of people does not necessarily identify the "network" relating people to people.

If networks were imagined as connecting lines, they would vary in darkness or weight. Strong network lines within the immediate family would appear heavy or dark. Network lines between employees and business associates might be medium weight, yet these, too, would be fairly distinct due to the common work hours and interdependence. Lighter, weaker lines would tie casual acquaintances and those persons encountered on an infrequent basis. Light or broken lines may characterize family relationships which are neglected.

Prior to the industrial and technological revolutions, the development of networks among people was much more closely defined. In rural, pre-industrial America, the networking among people was limited to distances easily traveled by foot or horseback.

The difficulty of communicating across long distances kept the networks near the geographic center of activity. Families tended to remain in the same areas for generations: grandparents, aunts, uncles and cousins were known in the community. Each individual was accepted in the context of immediate family and lineage. Life was lived in a close-knit, seldom-changing circle of persons who related to one another on several levels: family, labor, barter, recreation and religion. Networks were strong, easily identified and understood. Virtually all important communication was carried out face-to-face.

However, those days are past. Networking is now more complex. It has important implications for church strategies which address the Great Commission.

Networking in the community

Every community develops its unique system of networking. Consequently it is impossible to approach the concept of community networking with a simplistic design for every situation. However, communities have certain networking characteristics in common.

The suburban community

The advent of metroplex communities, commuter mass transportation and instant worldwide telephone and computer communication has revolutionized the network dynamic.

People who live next door to one another—as those densely grouped in apartments and condominiums—do not know one another. Often their networks are job-related and exist a great distance from their suburban communities. They spend the best part of the day in constant communication with co-workers who may live an hour's drive in the opposite direction. Daily these commuters invest their time and social energies in work. When husbands and wives carpool, it stretches their day from 6 a.m. to 6 p.m. Then they return home at night and on weekends to hibernate in apartments, condominiums and houses. They feel alone in the midst of multitudes, devoid of neighborhood networks.

Suburban shopping also reinforces the feeling of anonymity. Repeated trips to the grocery store remain encounters with unnamed people and unfamiliar faces. In shopping centers—hubs of great metropolitan regions—regular visits produce few networking relationships. The typical suburban dweller neither knows, nor is known by, those who live around him.

Neighborhood networks may be virtually non-existent, yet people do not live in a vacuum. Their network has simply expanded to a world community. A commuter may work all day with co-laborers who live in other parts of the metropolitan area. A salesman may communicate daily by telephone with persons in Los Angeles, Boston, New York, Philadelphia and Houston. An executive may commute weekly to these distant cities. For these persons, closer relationships may develop with people on either side of the continent than with those who live across the street.

The church planted in a pre-industrial, pre-technological age found ready root and fertile soil among the myriad community networks. But the church planted in today's suburban fringe discovers the soil stony and resistant. Churches on the suburban fringe may interpret as spiritual indifference what is actually a sociologic symptom. Network relationships have stretched beyond, and have formed outside the traditional community. In this context, the church must provide networks for people who are starved to know and be known by those who live closest to them.

The rural community

Networking in the rural community is more similar to the networking of traditional America. If the community is small enough, virtually everyone is known by name. One young woman recently moved from a metropolitan home to a small town, mused that her child returned from a neighborhood store reporting with disbelief: "Mother,

> *Network relationships have stretched beyond the traditional community. In this context, the church must provide networks for people who are starved to know and be known.*

they knew my name!"

Networks in these communities have been reinforced if not for centuries, certainly for generations. While this produces strongly defined network lines within the community, the network can also become inflexible or closed. Newcomers, quickly known by face and name (which may appear to be acceptance into the community network), may discover admittance is gained the "old fashioned way." They must earn it. This may not be accomplished in less than a generation if anyone not born in that community remains a "newcomer." It is possible for a longtime resident to live perpetually outside the networks of "real" residents.

In these communities, new residents may not be reached by older churches with strongly established leadership patterns. Some may be assimilated. More could be reached by new churches with new networking opportunities.

While suburban networking is virtually non-existent, where it does exist it is more open than its stronger rural counterpart.

Contrary to popular opinion, the inner city is not a community. It is a composite of many communities formed by various socio-economic and ethnic dimensions.

The inner city

Students of metropolitan development are well aware that metropolitan regions have grown outward from the center, like growth rings on a tree. In fact, these "growth rings" help define a city. As a city grows, it is forced to develop transportation "loops" for commerce. In Dallas, it was first loop 12, then 635; in Los Angeles it is 405, Santa Monica Freeway, Golden State Freeway and Ventura Freeway; in Chicago it is 294 and 90; in Kansas City it is 435 and 35. These major transportation loops often become distinguishable barriers between the heaving inner city within its circle and the suburban sprawl beyond.

From reflective highrise office buildings to the bustling economy springing up along the loop, the city is traversed by major freeways and thousands of commuters who never see the inner city. The inner city's dynamic mosaic of people is unknown, misunderstood and distrusted.

Contrary to popular opinion, the inner city is not a community. It is a composite of many communities, each formed by various socio-economic and ethnic dimensions. It contains distinct communities of people: Black, Hispanic, Chinese, Korean, Laotian, Vietnamese, Anglo, Japanese and others. Alongside these ethnic communities are those who have owned their homes for decades and who have watched their neighborhoods inundated by change. Like emerald islands in a heaving sea, these communities often consist of landscaped lawns surrounding mansions. Neighboring sections may have expensive, high-rise condominiums.

A drive through the city reveals its contrast and variety. Signs, advertisements, shops, restaurants and housing change as if a page were turned in a book. From block to block, from complex to complex, distinguishable communities exist side by side. Within these communities networking occurs.

A single apartment complex may house 2,000 to 3,000 people, a population the size of a rural city. These communities need churches for their unique socio-economic and ethnic populations.

Networking and the church

Heretofore, churches have viewed their "field" in geographic terms, often drawing a two-mile radius to determine their area of responsibility, their turf. When residents within that circle are visited by "outside" churches it may be viewed as an intrusion. However people do not necessarily attend churches along geographic lines. When "Sam Jones" trusts Christ as Savior and joins Trinity Church, he invites others to visit his newfound Christian family. He may have an aunt, uncle or cousin living in a distant neighborhood, but they are apt to attend church with Sam and find faith where he found it. The same thing will be true concerning those who work with Sam. As a result, persons living in the shadow of First Church may drive several miles to attend Trinity Church, while others drive past the conveniently located Trinity Church to attend First Church.

Church members may feel dismayed to discover that they do not reach the people who live close to the church building. But the church should consider this in the context of network dynamics. A church will most likely reach people through established network patterns.

Responses to questionnaires (completed by people attending church) indicated that family and friends are the

From block to block, from complex to complex, distinguishable communities exist side by side. Within these communities networking occurs.

strong est influence on where a person attends church. Very few indicated the influence of pastoral visits; less influential were revivals, buildings or programs. These factors are important to the life of a church, but are not perceived as the deciding factors for church attendance. Churches are made alive and effective by the living networks of people.

The description of the church field in geographic terms is no longer accurate. Churches grow along existing lines of communication and influence inherent in relationships among people. Lines of church growth are demographic rather than geographic. This principle is demonstrated in Paul's experience at Corinth. He effectively discipled Priscilla and Aquila who were tentmakers with him. But the couple had no natural networks since they had recently moved to Corinth from Rome. Rapid growth in the church at Corinth did not occur until Crispus, ruler of the synagogue, was converted. Thereafter "many of the Corinthians when they heard were believing and being baptized" (Acts 18:8). The network relationships opened up by the conversion of Crispus gave the young church the channels along which it could reach many people rapidly.

Churches will be more effective in their own growth if they discover where the networks of their people exist, and capitalize upon these to reach others for Christ.

Because churches grow along network lines, churches can exist in close proximity to each other and yet reach an entirely different network of people.

Because churches grow along network lines, churches can exist in close proximity to each other and yet reach an entirely different network of people. Churches need to be planted according to the unreached networks of people which exist in a community rather than by the location of pins on a map.

Networking in the Christian sub-culture

Those who have been raised in the church may depend upon networking developed within a Christian subculture. Having recently moved to a suburban area, a family seeks out a church, expecting it to provide networking in their community. With church programs for youth and children, women's and men's organizations, recreational, devotional and service opportunities, the family finds its networking needs met among Christians who have similar interests and values.

Churches precisely structure their organizations and programs to reach this particular "church oriented" family. As a result, the vast majority of recorded "church growth" is transfer growth produced by the mobility of Christian families. This gives rise to the creation of a "Christian subculture" in which families and individuals continue to move in the same circles.

The "church culture" does not have a strong network among the non-Christian segment of the world. While members of this church culture are willing to work in the secular environment, they view themselves as separate, and readily retreat to the safe networks of the church community.

In practical terms, the church does not view the vast, non-Christian population of the world as viable "prospects" for membership. Churches consider the Christian subculture as their "market," and view additional churches as competitors. For this reason, established churches often times resist the planting of new churches within their community.

New churches, however, are much more likely to reach non-Christians and assimilate them into the life of the church. While they have fewer programs to offer, these new churches reach people with the gospel, challenging men and women to seek a vision for the future and offering them an opportunity for sacrifice.

The existence of the Christian subculture, together with modern tools of communication, has given rise to a unique phenomenon: a Christian culture that stretches across denominational lines.

The modern Christian culture has created its own electronic church. It has produced its own Christian yellow pages and advertising which encourages even closer networking and separation from the world. It has its celebrities and entertainers. It has produced its own counselors, with Christian counseling centers in almost every major city, and counselors via radio, tape, television and film. While these do not represent an official organization, they are representative of a particular Christian-based "culture" in our society. The expanded network of people may explain the success enjoyed by the electronic church which links thousands of homes and stretches across a wide geographic area. Yet the impact of this medium in terms of making new disciples is limited. It primarily provides a "one way" network system to those already within the Christian community and substitutes for interpersonal relationships formed within the neighborhood. Although some evangelism results, its total impact is relatively small within the secular networks of the world.

Networking and church growth

Understanding networking enables the church to funnel more effectively its energies into areas that will produce growth. A church which recognizes that growth occurs along lines of personal influence among its members can begin using its best channel for reaching people.

A church with members who enjoy many networks within the community is a church that has great potential for growth. A church that has grown inward, so that all the members are related to one another, is a church that has become root bound. Its established networks may create resistance to the very things that foster church growth. A church should recognize that each new member and each new convert brings into the church new opportunities for reaching people with the gospel of Christ. These dynamics are related to the issues discussed in the chapter on growth. Organizational expansion must take place to make room for new networks within the congregation.

Churches reach a plateau in growth because the network potential within the congregation is saturated—even though the church exists in the midst of thousands of non-Christians. When this occurs, the best alternative is found in the creation of new units and in the creation of new churches.

Networking and new churches

Communities which afford opportunities for creation and maintenance of new networks are fertile soil for new churches. This would be true of a rapidly growing single family suburban neighborhood that is isolated from surrounding suburban and metropolitan communities. Such a neighborhood could be populated by many new residents anxious to establish new relationships with new neighbors. The public school system, the emerging recreation organizations, volunteer service groups and developing city government could provide rapidly expanding networks through which people interact, and through which the church may grow.

> *Churches reach a plateau because the network potential within the congregation is saturated—even though the church exists in the midst of thousands of non-Christians.*

Inner-city communities also provide remarkably fertile soil for planting churches. Many inner-city communities are composed of distinct ethnic and cultural groups that have developed strong networks. Seeing themselves as a minority culture, be it Laotian, Cambodian, Vietnamese, Black or Hispanic, they often have developed an interdependent network for survival. Drawn together by language and culture, these communities often include large families with many relationships. Once the gospel has penetrated the network, it often experiences rapid communication and acceptance.

Rural communities may also offer fertile soil for a new congregation, while established churches have developed closed networks. Patriarchs of the community maintain decision-making positions within the church. Newer residents may have only limited influence even after years of faithful involvement.

Within these communities, there may exist an entire population that is beyond the reach of the established congregation yet could be reached and discipled by a new church. New churches offer open networks that can rapidly assimilate members. A young congregation is eager to accept new members into the life of the church, to offer opportunities for service, leadership and friendship.

A new congregation retains a higher percentage of new members than does the more established congregation. The older church may receive as many or even more new members, but will likely lose these within a relatively short time.

Total penetration with the gospel of Christ will not occur through churches that reach a reasonable percentage of a large geographic area but by churches that can penetrate every networking dimension of the world.

Churches may be needed in penthouses of multi-million dollar condominiums, in mobile home parks, apartment complexes, government subsidized housing units, as well as suburban communities and rural villages.

Those of the first-century church recognized the importance of networking and carefully recorded the names of key individuals who offered access to the greater networks of people. Andrew and Peter were brothers. James and John were both sons of Zebedee and companions of Peter and Andrew in the fishing industry of Capernaum.

Philip was also "from the city of Andrew and Peter," and he found Nathanael, saying, "We have found Him of whom Moses in the law and also the prophets wrote" (John 1:45). Mary, Martha and Lazarus were siblings in the city of Bethany. At the crucifixion, Jesus Christ's own mother Mary was accompanied by the mother of James and John, the wife of Zebedee. It was Christ's half-brother James who became the leader of the church at Jerusalem.

In the book of Acts, Sergius Paulus, as proconsul on Cyprus, had access to networks of relationship throughout the island.

> *A new church offers open networks that can rapidly assimilate members. A young congregation is eager to accept new members into the life of the church.*

The apostle Paul concluded his letter to the Romans by identifying the key persons then at Rome who formed the network through which Rome was being discipled: "Greet Prisca and Aquila, my fellow workers in Christ Jesus, who for my life risked their own necks, to whom not only do I give thanks, but also all the churches of the Gentiles; also greet the church that is in their house. Greet Epaenetus, my beloved, who is the first convert to Christ from Asia. Greet Mary, who has worked hard for you. Greet Andronicus and Junias, my kinsmen, and my fellow prisoners, who are outstanding among the apostles, who also were in Christ before me. Greet Ampliatus, my beloved in the Lord. Greet Urbanus, our fellow worker in Christ, and Stachys my beloved. Greet Apelles, the approved in Christ. Greet those who are of the household of Aristobulus. Greet Herodion, my kinsman. Greet those of the household of Narcissus, who are in the Lord. Greet Tryphaena and Tryphosa, workers in the Lord. Greet Persis, the beloved, who has worked hard in the Lord. Greet Rufus, a choice man in the Lord, also his mother and mine. Greet Asyncritus, Phlegon, Hermes, Patrobas, Hermas, and the brethren with them. Greet Philologus and Julia, Nereus and his sister, and Olympas, and all the saints who are with them" (Rom. 16:3-15, NASB).

Such lists of difficult names in the Scripture are oftentimes glossed over as meaningless. But the message within this "incidental" record is critical. Here are the personal network keys that unlocked Rome! The abundance of Greek and Roman names is obvious.

It should be noted that Priscilla and Aquila, who in Acts 18 had recently arrived from Rome, had at this time traveled full circle and returned to the Roman capital. They must have maintained many friends and acquaintances who became natural channels for the spread of the gospel. The New International Commentary on Romans cites J.B. Lightfoot's contention that Apelles of verse 10 "was a grandson of Herod the Great and of Agrippa and of Herod (king of Chalcis) and on intimate relations with the Emperor Claudius." An elaborate and natural network of relationships must have existed throughout the great city of Rome as these, their households and friends, were discipling people to Christ.

Conclusion

The church has always grown, and will continue to grow, along the lines of network relationships. Whenever an attempt is made to grow in any other way, growth becomes artificial and inevitably meets with defeat at the point of discipling through congregations. If the church will be successful in fulfilling the Great Commission of Christ, it must discover the means of penetrating the existing networks of human relations and plant congregations within the framework of each. It must discover the dynamics of networking within the local congregation and capitalize upon these principles.

Questions for pastors and churches:

1. What are the networks within my congregation?
2. Are these networks saturated?
3. How could my church be structured so that its networks would be more open to the assimilation of new members?
4. What are the networks within my community?
5. What networks do the members of my church have within the community?
6. How could the gospel be communicated by the members of my church through existing networks?
7. How could the church help develop better networking in the community?
8. Is my church structured to reach those of the Christian subculture only?
9. How could my church be structured to penetrate the secular networks of the community?
10. Could our church plant new churches within particular networking segments of the community?

The church has always grown, and will continue to grow, along the lines of network relationships. The church must capitalize on these relationships.

THE
Indig

enous

DIMENSION

I f a mission is to become an autonomous congregation, it must be an indigenous work, growing naturally within its context. Otherwise it will probably remain a dependent ministry of another congregation, able to add to the kingdom perhaps, but unable to multiply. More than any other aspect of church planting, the indigenous dimension determines success or failure.

Culture

The concept of indigenous work complements the ethnic dimension, yet is broader in application. Webster defines the word indigenous as "produced, growing, or living naturally in a particular region or environment." The word applies to plants and animals which are native to a particular part of the world. A camel indigenous to desert regions could not survive in arctic tundra. A walrus of the North would die quickly in a hot, arid climate.

Human beings are indigenous to particular regions—and cultural climates. When people from a distinct sociological/ethnic group immigrate to a new region, they take with them the culture. They thrive within their context of language, religion, values and art. Each ethnic group contains cultural groups reflecting further distinctions of custom, dress, and habits of sleeping and eating.

Often the gospel fails to penetrate a particular group because the message is identified with cultural values rather than with the Christian faith. The Anglo wedding ceremony is not taken from Scripture. A minister must turn to etiquette and pastoral handbooks for prescribed marriage ceremonies. The Bible is silent concerning this and other ceremonies of birth, death and worship.

According to the indigenous principle, the gospel may find a variety of cultural expressions without compromising the message of the crucified and resurrected Christ. In the light of Scripture, Cambodians may celebrate marriage, continue their diet, bury their dead and conduct worship as only Cambodians can do. The same holds true for Anglos, Koreans, Hispanics, Laotians, Japanese, Chinese, Ethiopians, Romanians, etc. Only as the body of Christ expands to include all cultures of this complex society will the strategy of Jesus be fulfilled and the peoples of this world discipled.

However, definition of the indigenous dimension reaches beyond culture. Churches may be started within any culture and incorporate aspects of the culture—yet still fail to be indigenous.

Only as the body of Christ expands to include all cultures of this complex society will the strategy of Jesus be fulfilled and the peoples of this world discipled.

Ownership

If mission work is to succeed, all aspects of ownership must shift from the sponsoring group into the hands of those who comprise the mission congregation.

This issue must be handled with sensitivity, particularly in the areas of leadership and resources. Without leaders from "among the people," the mission congregation will struggle and perhaps die. A mission largely funded by outside sources for an extended time will become a disabled limb in the body of Christ.

Leadership and resources

The successful mission enterprise of the first century is

marked by indigenous leaders and resources. The Antioch mission effort was not a plan to transfer Antiochian Christians to Cyprus, Iconium, Lystra, Philippi, Thessalonica and Corinth. Nor was it a financial extension of the mother church. Rather, each mission effort would be indigenous in terms of leaders and resources.

As Paul, Barnabas and John Mark watched the mountain ranges of Cyprus rise above the sparkling Mediterranean, they must have wondered how this first church-planting expedition would unfold. They must have seen the large commercial harbor of Salamis and its populated shores as both opportunity and obstacle. It was not until they had made their way the length of the island that the Scripture pauses to identify their success.

Sergius Paulus, proconsul on the island of Cyprus, "a man of intelligence," became a significant leader and contributor to the church established there by Paul and Barnabas. An inscription dated A.D. 52-53 uncovered at the city of Paphos bears the words: "in the time of proconsul Paulus." This man, otherwise a mere name on an ancient inscription, became a permanently recorded participant in the Cyprian church.

Years later the Apostle Paul followed his "Macedonian vision" into the proud city of Philippi, the "miniature Rome." Philippi boasted no strong synagogue. But a small band of Jews worshiped on the banks of the Angista river. In this quiet setting of fragrant grass and babbling waters, came the first convert. The environment seemed appropriate for one like Lydia. This gentle lady was also a businesswoman, a seller of purple fabrics. She was comfortable not only in the quiet setting where Paul found her, but amid the barter and rush of the marketplace. Lydia provided that first strategic piece in the indigenous mosaic that became the Philippian church.

The second piece in this mosaic was an unlikely candidate: a Roman soldier charged with the task of imprisoning state criminals. He was probably better acquainted with the dark recesses of an underground prison than with the sunlit countryside; his ears more attuned to verbal abuse from incarcerated and tortured men. He may have appeared callous and cold. But in a moment of despair he asked the pivotal question: "Sirs, what must I do to be saved?"

These two, Lydia and the jailer, along with their households and a growing company of others, formed the indigenous church which would later receive Paul's letter of joy.

Alone, Paul came to the "eye of Greece," metropolitan Corinth, located on a narrow isthmus connecting Achaia with the European continent.

With the Acrocorinthus Rock rising 1,750 feet above the city, this crossroads of commerce for the Roman world portrayed natural beauty and human squalor. Excavations reveal 33 nightclubs in this center of moral degeneracy in the Greco-Roman world.

Paul invested months of patient cultivation before winning his first converts, the young couple Priscilla and Aquila, who had recently arrived from Rome. The Scripture simply states that Paul stayed with them because he shared their trade, tent making. We may imagine long relaxed hours of conversation as they cut, measured and sewed tents for market. Out of this relationship, two devout Jews became ardent believers in the risen Christ. They would not only form a critical part of the Corinthian church, but at Ephesus they would instruct the eloquent Apollos.

> *Paul invested months of patient cultivation before winning his first converts. Out of this relationship, two devout Jews became ardent believers in the risen Christ.*

Soon added to their number was Titius Justus, a Greek proselyte to Judaism who embraced the Christian faith. His house became the base for a strategic operation next door to the synagogue.

The key, however, to the Corinthian church growth seems to have been Crispus, the leader of the synagogue. After Crispus embraced Christianity, his family "and many of the Corinthians when they heard, were believing and being baptized" (Acts 18:8). These became the indigenous base for both leadership and resources in the Corinthian church.

Sergius Paulus, Jason, Priscilla, Aquila, Titius Justus, Crispus, Lydia, the jailer and the elders, all were from the communities and regions where churches were being planted. Importing leaders from one community to the other would have limited the outreach of the early church.

Indigeneity and contemporary missions

How does the indigenous principle affect current strategies for missions? Many older churches are reluctant to start a mission church of similar socio-economic character. They are afraid they must send out a large number of their members to start the new congregation. Would-be mission pastors are afraid to begin new work without involvement of a substantial nucleus from a sponsoring church.

But according to the indigenous principle, a mission will begin and grow much more effectively with the help of only a few sponsoring members, compatible with people living in the target area.

Occasionally mission work is begun with a significant number of members drawn from the mother church. If these persons are already closely related to one another, and especially if they do not live in the target area, the church may soon find itself in the throes of spiritual abortion.

One recent mission effort was begun by the sponsoring church sending out a large group of its members. The target was a community adjacent to that of the sponsor church. Both were middleclass and upper-middleclass Anglo communities. However, the target community was composed primarily of younger professional and upwardly mobile adults. From its own community, the mother church sent 35 older adults. On the first Sunday, 45 persons attended; one year later, the mission was averaging 30 in Sunday School. The mission is struggling against the indigenous current. It will likely not grow until its leaders and the majority of its members are derived from the target area.

When a large number of mature Christian adults is enlisted to begin a new congregation, oddly enough its ability to reach the unchurched is reduced. Those with a non-Christian orientation are confused by the accepted religious terms and concepts. New Christians need classes with basic discussions about Christianity in language that is free of religious jargon.

When I moved to The Colony, Texas, to organize a church, we printed a brochure. It stated that the pastor had "moved onto the field." That failed to communicate to the unchurched of the community. It should have said the pastor had "moved into the city," then they would have understood.

As The Colony congregation grew, it attracted a large number of young electrical engineers. I struggled with their professional jargon and toured manufacturing plants to learn more about "hardware," "software" and "silicon chips."

The unchurched person faces a similar communication breakdown as pastor and members talk about the "millennia," the "parousia," "Judaizers," Saul, Paul and three different Johns, Simon, Peter and Cephas. Even the Old and New Testaments, Exodus and the Pentateuch sound foreign. Yet long-time church members may bandy about these terms with no further thought or explanation.

A church structured with new converts in roles of leadership may be less stable, yet these people likely will attract others from the world more quickly and easily. New churches serve best when they focus on the lost, unenlisted and uninvolved.

Each congregation must be allowed to adopt the cultural expressions of its people; ownership must be sensitively nurtured; congregations must enlist new converts and the unchurched for positions of leadership. Resources must spring from the discipling of the people within the mission effort.

hose with a non-Christian orientation are confused by the accepted religious terms and concepts. New Christians need classes in language that is free of religious jargon.

Questions for pastors and churches:

1. Is our church indigenous to the people?

2. What are the cultural expressions of our church that make it indigenous?

3. Do our people feel a sense of ownership in the church?

4. Does our church sponsor a mission?

5. If so, are we allowing the mission to be indigenous?

6. Are we allowing the mission congregation to assume "ownership" in terms of resources and leadership?

7. Could we delegate to the mission congregation more responsibility for leadership and resources?

ach congregation must be allowed to adopt the cultural expressions of its people. Resources must spring from the discipling of the people within the mission effort.

THE Har

DIMENSION

W e live in an age of religious affluence. Many churches have million-dollar budgets. Denominations and religious organizations own and operate entire communications networks and publishing houses. Billions of dollars are donated to religious causes. The resources of the modern church are great. Yet in face of the need, the resources seem inadequate. Only one resource is virtually inexhaustible in terms of reaching a lost world. And that is the harvest.

Resources in the harvest

When Jesus with his disciples stood adjacent to Jacob's well and beheld the multitude of Samaritans, he had at his disposal a meager treasury entrusted to Judas. The twelve had just returned from a journey into the nearby village where they had frugally purchased bread for the journey. The statement they heard from the Master would later revolutionize their thinking with respect to resources. "Lift up your eyes, and look on the fields; for they are white already to harvest" (John 4:35). Jesus was speaking of people. Many students of the Bible believe that he was referring directly to the crowds of Samaritan men cresting the horizon in quest of the one whom the adulterous woman called Messiah.

When Jesus spoke of the fields, he identified the harvest as the urgent need—as well as the great resource.

As easily, Jesus could have said of the people, "Look on the fields for they are *fertile already to sow.*" That, however, would have required that the seed be provided by the sowers. And this would have robbed the statement of its full implication. A field ripe for harvest is full of the seeds that will produce future crops. The imagery is critical as the church of the 20th century seeks its place in the harvest strategy of God.

Christ's assignment to the 70 disciples as recorded in Luke is an object lesson in the harvest principle. As he sent these fearful disciples into every city and village, he specifically instructed them regarding resources: "Carry no purse, no bag, no shoes. . . . And whatever house you enter, first say, 'Peace be to this house.'. . . And stay in that house, eating and drinking what they give you, for the laborer is worthy of his wages. . . . And whatever city you enter, and they receive you, eat what is set before you" (Luke 10:4-8, NASB).

Why did Jesus advocate such austerity for these 70 disciples? He must have been concerned that they discover the harvest principle. And that would be impossible if they took adequate provisions. His teaching aim is stated in Luke 10:2, "The harvest is plentiful, but the laborers are few." The hindrance to the Great Commission has never been inadequate financial resources. All the financial resources are provided in the harvest itself.

Hindrances to the harvest

Hindrances to accomplishing the Great Commission focus on the laborers. They have not been sent. Men and women who could gather the crops, find themselves in the barns and grainbins re-arranging the yield of past harvests while white fields rot. Too many churches are afraid of releasing their members to missions, afraid of a weakened

A field ripe for harvest is full of the seeds that will produce future crops. The imagery is critical as the church of the 20th century seeks its place in the harvest strategy of God.

home base, lagging budget and attendance. Too quickly, too easily and too often a "save-the-institution" mentality suffocates the adventurous mission spirit. Many laypersons would readily respond to sacrificial missions if church leaders would boldly issue the call. Until that happens, there will be no national or worldwide awakening. Until then, the harvest will be neglected for want of laborers.

Does this reflect some failure on the part of the Lord of the harvest? Jesus Christ's parable about the hiring of laborers at every hour of the day is evidence of his constant seeking of those who will gather his harvest into the storehouse.

The church has not seen its resources through the eyes of God. "Our resources are small and the need is so great," the church says, trembling. "How can our little bit make any difference?" Church budgets are already strained. To support another mission seems out of the question. Yet only when a concerted effort is made to meet a definite need are resources multiplied. Is that not at the heart of Christ's feeding the 5,000 and the 4,000? His power to multiply resources became evident only after the sacrificial offering of a few loaves and fishes.

In faithfully attempting to meet the need, God's people fed the hungry multitude, and a surplus of 12 baskets of food was gathered afterward.

Risk in the harvest

Jesus links risk with the concept of harvest in his statement of Luke 10, "The harvest is plentiful, but the laborers are few, therefore beseech the Lord of the harvest to send out laborers into his harvest. Go your ways, I send you out as lambs in the midst of wolves."

Jesus clearly taught his 70 followers that missions, world evangelism and spiritual awakening always involve risk. These 70 would embark upon a journey into strange regions without purse, bag or shoes, without cash, credit cards, telephone, transportation or contacts for lodging. They began their journey, penniless, trusting only in the counsel of Jesus that the resource is in the harvest.

Laborers must be sent. That still entails risk. Without church leaders and laity who are risk-takers, the harvest will remain in the fields, and multitudes will enter eternity without Christ.

> *Jesus clearly taught his 70 followers that missions, world evangelism and spiritual awakening always involve risk. They began their journey penniless.*

61

Churches must give sacrificially, then trust God for multiplication of their resources. Churches must be willing to risk everything instead of focusing on survival. Jesus said, "He that would save his life shall lose it, but he that would lose his life for my sake and the gospel's shall find it." His life expressed this principle.

In rare instances, men will sacrifice self-interest for the sake of others. On January 13, 1982, the ill-fated Air Florida flight 90 began its take off from Washington's National Airport. The scream of straining jet engines could be heard as the aircraft shuddered in a desperate attempt to lift its ice-laden fuselage. Carrying 79 passengers, it plunged into the icy waters of the Potomac River. As the helicopter returned repeatedly to rescue survivors—one at a time—from the deadly cold waters, America witnessed an heroic display of sacrifice. The life ring tethered to the helicopter was thrown to Arland Williams, a 46-year-old bank examiner, but he passed it to another.

Having pulled that victim from the water, the rescue copter returned in minutes to throw the life ring once again to Williams. Although visibly weakening in the freezing water, he passed the ring to another.

Returning a third time, the helicopter crew searched for the familiar form. Officer Gene Windsor, one of the two-man helicopter rescue crew, wept as he described their experience. "He could have gone on the first trip," stated the pilot, Donald Usher, "but he put everyone else ahead of himself. Everyone."

The blades of the chopper rippled the water with its icy wind. The vision of that empty surface sent chills of awe and sadness through the hearts of millions. What a graphic expression of Romans 5:7, "Very rarely will anyone die for a righteous man, though for a good man someone might possibly dare to die."

The kind of sacrifice exhibited by Arland Williams must capture the heart of the church. Christians of the 20th and 21st centuries must turn their backs on survivalist instinct and labor sacrificially if the people of the world are to be saved.

Laity

Risk for the laity may involve loss of established church support systems, worship with family and friends and

> *Churches must give sacrificially, then trust God for multiplication of their resources. Churches must be willing to risk everything instead of focusing on survival.*

specialized programs. Rather than opt for prestige of leadership in established churches, lay men and women must respond to the challenge of reaping where others have not reaped, building where no buildings exist and planning where programs are needed.

Clergy

During the 1980s, a record number of students enrolled in seminaries and theological institutions. Today the number of graduates is greater than the number of churches without pastors. So these young people need training with a view for missions. They need models who are risk-takers for the kingdom. Otherwise these God-called laborers will sit, disillusioned, in the sun. They will be unable to find the harvest.

Prior to my first experience as mission pastor, I labored in two well established congregations. In both situations, the risk factor was low. As long as I preached on Sunday and remained morally true, the members would continue to attend as they had for decades.

A mission church posed an entirely different situation for me. Unless I did something positive and right, the mission effort would "dry up and blow away." Mere maintenance ministry would not do.

Simply to keep the seven persons who began that congregation would have left me red-faced before my peers and Christ—like the steward who hid his one talent in the earth so that it might not be lost. Instead, I was forced to perform as a five- or three-talent steward of Jesus Christ's parable; in order to gain, I had to risk the loss of that which I had been given.

Will church leaders stand ashamedly before Christ, having opted for security, having failed to invest our God-given resources?

All of the resources necessary for world evangelism are in the harvest; but the fields will never be harvested without laborers who are willing to RISK!

Churches

Scripture teaches sacrificial living—the church accepts its historical demonstration in the life of Jesus Christ. Yet the church embraces a survivalist mentality. The principles which govern individual believers are the principles which

*S*cripture teaches sacrificial living—the church accepts its historical demonstration in the life of Jesus Christ. Yet the church embraces a survivalist mentality.

bring life or death in the corporate body. When the church turns inward and is more concerned with survival than sacrifice, it is courting decline and death. From the core, it begins to rot. The thrill of commitment is lost. Motivation for outreach becomes distorted as church visitors and new residents become "prospects" for financial support and perpetuation of the institution. The church turns its attention to unclaimed members of the denomination in hopes that their tithes and energy will help perpetuate survival of the church.

The church must embrace its death, that Christ might live. A congregation that risks its own survival to sponsor another church, sets in motion an interesting phenomenon. Life within the new mission becomes contagious. Soon the sponsor church is experiencing new life and new vision.

Churches must risk all in order to win some. They must refocus their energies on the waves of wheat ready for harvest.

Questions for pastors and churches:

1. Is our church more concerned about survival or kingdom expansion?

2. Does our church seek to reach people to strengthen the church, or does it seek to meet the spiritual needs of people?

3. What resources does our church have to assist in starting a new church?

4. How much of our church's resources would be required to start a new church?

5. Would God provide the resources for church starting through people reached by that effort?

6. Is our church willing to take the risk necessary for starting new churches?

7. Are there people in our church who would risk becoming the core of a new congregation?

8. Am I willing to take the risk to help start a new church?

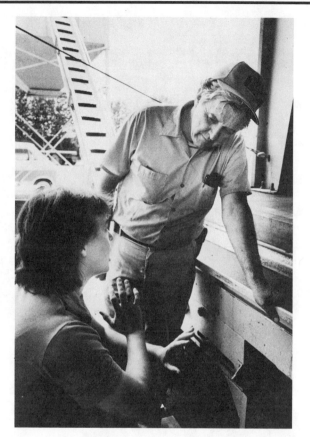

*T*he church must embrace its death, that Christ might live. Churches must risk all in order to win some.

THE
Lead

ership

DIMENSION

T hou art Peter, and upon this rock I will build my church."
Perhaps no statement of Jesus has been more critically
examined. Greek scholars put on their reading glasses, open
lexicons and dissect the sentence, case and gender. Jesus Christ's
choice for Peter, *petros*, is a Greek word in the masculine gender
meaning rock. Jesus chose the neuter *petra* to describe the rock
upon which he will build his church. Here, as on other occasions,
Jesus used a play on words to make a concept stick in the minds of
his followers.

The antecedent for petra is found in Peter's affirmation, "Thou
art the Christ, the Son of the living God." Faith in Jesus Christ is the
petra or basis of the church and this is crucial to our theological
understanding.

All who come to faith in Jesus Christ as the Son of the living God
are a part of his universal church. And within this Scripture verse

emerges another key element. When Jesus said, "Thou art Peter," he was affirming that his church would be inextricably linked with petros and its other leaders. Jesus emphasized the fact that people need leaders; they determine the heights to which a people will rise. Church leadership is crucial to the fulfillment of the Great Commission.

The difference of leadership

People need leaders; they determine the heights to which a people will rise. Church leadership is crucial to the fulfillment of the Great Commission.

Many churches sit dormant until the right leader arrives. More than buildings, location, population, history and tradition, leaders determine the future of a congregation.

Fifteen years ago the First Baptist Church of Houston, a congregation in the midst of the largest metropolitan center in Texas, was in rapid decline. About 400 people were worshiping in a sanctuary designed to seat 2,000. Buildings were neglected and deteriorating and the future looked dismal until the church called John Bisagno to be its pastor. In a short time, the trend was reversed. By 1983, attendance at FBC Houston was averaging almost 5,000. The difference is leadership.

In July of 1969, Tom Wolfe accepted the call of the Church on Brady Street in Los Angeles, California. It was a dying Anglo congregation in a transitional neighborhood; average attendance was 75. Members had considered selling the building and dissolving the church. They could not even guarantee the new pastor a regular salary.

Yet with determination and an uncompromising vision, Wolfe led the church in outreach and ministry to its community. Today, with 80 percent Hispanic members, the Church on Brady averages 650 in Sunday attendance, 400 on Wednesday evenings. It has the largest Hispanic membership of any church in the Southern Baptist General Convention of California. The difference is leadership.

In 1979, Charles and Dotty Brock, Southern Baptist missionaries to the Philippines, arrived in Manila, a metroplex of 10 million people. Brock walked through the northeast quarter of the city seeking those with an interest in Bible study. After four months, with 15 newly baptized members, a church was formed.

Within a short time, Tom Escota, a successful marble manufacturer, became a Christian and joined the church. Six months after it began, the church called Escota to be its pastor. In 1985, Pinyahan Baptist Church celebrated its fourth anniversary with 200 in attendance. Already it had started two other churches and had adopted a goal to start six more churches the next year.

Without denominational subsidy, now three churches exist where there was none. The difference is leadership.

Characteristics of leaders

Effective leaders possess clear goals. They know where they are going.

This is characteristic of the life of Jesus. When his mother was looking for him in the temple, Jesus' first recorded words declared a sense of priority: "Did you not know I must be about the things of my Father?" He responded to a plea for a miracle at the wedding feast of Cana: "Mine hour has not yet come." He knew his mission: "The Son of Man is come to seek and to save the lost."

Not even the prospects of suffering and death clouded his clear vision: "Now my soul is troubled, and what shall I say? Father, save me from this hour: but for this cause, came I into the world."

Nothing could turn Jesus from his goal, not family, friend or foe. He would accomplish the redemptive task for which he had come. His perfect life would be crushed. His spotless soul and spirit would be cast into the depths of hell to endure the ultimate separation and torment. But he willingly gave his life so that guilty men might be spared the consequences of their own sin. His goal was clear.

The Apostle Paul singlemindedly pursued his goal: "this one thing I do, forgetting those things which are behind, and reaching forth unto those things which are before, I press toward the mark for the prize of the high calling of God in Christ Jesus" (Phil. 3: 13,14).

His purpose is further delineated in his statements to the Corinthians: "For I determined not to know anything among you, save Jesus Christ and Him crucified."

Paul said concisely, "I am made all things to all men, that I might by all means save some." With a definite goal, Paul emerged a powerful leader of the first century church.

Whether it is Abraham Lincoln with his unswerving dedication to preserve the Union, or Winston Churchill with his commitment to victory at all costs, or Martin Luther King with his dream of racial equality—and whether it is verbalized, or not—effective leaders operate with clear, concise goals.

Effective leaders are able to conceive practical steps to accomplish their goals.

Deliberately and systematically, Jesus began his three-year ministry. He did not move randomly about the countryside passing time until his "hour should come." Each miracle, each parable, each action, each word was aimed at clarifying for humanity the divine will. Each day, each hour brought him closer to his purpose which culminated in death at Golgotha.

The Apostle Paul was concerned with his disciplined race to the goal: "I, therefore, so run, not as uncertainly; so fight I, not as one that beateth air" (1 Cor. 9:26). Acts recounts Paul's systematically planting churches in major metropolitan areas by entering the synagogues, dialoguing with priests, winning the "God fearers," and establishing a base of operation. While Paul worked, he discipled others to plant churches in other cities.

Effective leaders must be able to design effective plans as well as dream great dreams. Joseph, perhaps the greatest Old Testament dreamer, became Egypt's prime minister after demonstrating an ability to design strategies and reorganize men to implement those dreams.

To be effective, the church must have leaders who can take practical steps to accomplish their plans for church growth and to embrace the world with the gospel.

Effective leaders are able to transmit their vision to others and to enlist their help in achieving the goals.

A vision locked within a single mind cannot change the world. The idea must be communicated in such a way that it becomes the dream of others. It must be communicated in such practical ways that others will help make that shared dream a reality.

Jesus, the master-leader of men, communicated his dream. Men were willing to leave family, career and possessions to follow in the Kingdom pursuit. Although they did not understand his full-blown strategy, they wanted to join his spiritual revolution.

Paul successfully communicated his goals and dreams. Although his companions at Troas did not receive the Macedonian vision: "after he (Paul) had seen the vision, immediately we endeavored to go into Macedonia, assuredly gathering that the Lord had called us to preach the

> *E*ffective leaders are able to conceive practical steps to accomplish their goals. Effective leaders are able to transmit their vision to others and enlist their help in achieving the goals.

gospel unto them" (Acts 16:10). As he continued his missionary enterprise, the list of those challenged by Paul grew to include Timothy, Titus, Silas, Luke, Priscilla, Aquila, Lydia, Justus, Crispus, Jason and Tertius.

For spiritual awakening to sweep the world, God must raise up men with a vision for total world evangelism, a grasp for the right methods to accomplish that end and the ability to inspire others to follow.

Effective leaders are willing to take risk.

Leadership is always risky business. Martin Luther risked defeat and death when he launched the Reformation. William Carey risked livelihood and safety when he quit his job and left his home to become a missionary to India. But his risk marked the start of the modern missionary movement.

Jesus taught risk. Through parables he encouraged his disciples to risk all for the pearl of great price, for the treasure hidden in the field. Through example he showed his followers how to jeopardize reputation and life for a worthy cause.

Some can dream dreams. They can devise workable plans for accomplishing those dreams. They can motivate others to help make the dreams reality. But if they lack the will to risk, these gifted people will never be leaders.

Questions for pastors and churches:

1. What are the leadership qualities of our pastor?
2. Does my church have a distinct goal for the future?
3. Has my church formulated specific plans to reach its goal?
4. Are members motivated to pursue the church goals through a unified plan of action?
5. Am I willing to take the risks necessary to lead my church?
6. Is our church willing to take the risks necessary to disciple more people?
7. If our church is searching for a pastor, what are the leadership qualities we are looking for?
8. If our church is sponsoring a mission, what kind of leader do we need for its pastor?
9. Do lay people in my church possess leadership gifts?
10. How can the leadership qualities of key lay people be enlisted for the growth of our church?

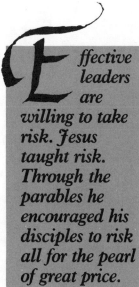

ffective leaders are willing to take risk. Jesus taught risk. Through the parables he encouraged his disciples to risk all for the pearl of great price.

THE
Plan

ning DIMENSION

J esus Christ's statement to Peter reflects a strategy for warfare when he says of the church, "The gates of Hell shall not prevail against it." To expand that imagery, Satan is besieged in his fortress of darkness. With supply lines cut off, his retreat blocked, he trembles behind locked doors as battering rams of light pound the gates. It is the climax of the battle.

It evokes visions of a despairing Hitler trapped in his bunker, listening to the relentless pounding of allied bombs that shook the concrete walls of his underground sanctuary. This perpetrator of the holocaust did not come to this end accidentally. Months of strategy and coordinated efforts by the allied forces led to the ultimate defeat of this crazed and powerful ruler who pushed humanity to the brink of destruction.

The church must likewise carry out its onslaught against Satan's kingdom with a coordinated effort employing all its forces in a well-planned strategy for victory. For the church to do otherwise would be disastrous.

Jesus talked in terms of a battle plan in another illustration: "What king, going to make war against another king, sitteth not down first, and consulteth whether he be able with ten thousand to meet him that cometh against him with twenty thousand? Or else while the other is yet a great way off, he sendeth an ambassage, and desireth conditions of peace?" (Luke 14:31-32). Although he was explaining the necessity to count the cost of discipleship, Jesus was also teaching the importance of wise planning.

The goal to be achieved by his strategy, the discipling of the nations, will continue to elude the church until it employs adequate planning.

Planning in the ministry of Paul

The Apostle Paul emphasized the importance of planning in his statement to the Corinthians, "according to the grace of God which is given unto me, as a wise masterbuilder, I have laid the foundation, and another buildeth thereon."

Paul's choice of words here is instructive. His words which are translated as wise masterbuilder, *sophos arketekton*, could be translated "wise architect."

In the architectural profession, each well-executed project requires weeks of study and preparation. Building custom homes on steep cliffs, the architect must work to convert rough, unfriendly terrain into a habitable place with aesthetic grace. To plan towering skyscrapers, he must calculate not only the effect of his building upon those surrounding it, but he must consider the effect of those buildings upon his own design.

Utilities, foundation, engineering, appearance, access and egress are planned. Details must be carefully drafted before the first shovel of dirt is turned. Even so must the *sophos arketekton* of the kingdom approach the task of world evangelism through the multiplication of churches.

Acts makes it clear that Paul did not approach church starting haphazardly.

Acts 16 reveals the struggle engaged by the Apostle as he sought to develop his strategy. The Scripture simply states, "When they had gone throughout Phrygia and the region of Galatia, and were forbidden of the Holy Spirit to preach the word in Asia, after they were come to Mysia, they assayed to go into Bithynia: but the Spirit suffered them not. And they passing by Mysia came down to Troas" (Acts 16:6-8). It·was there, of course, that Paul and his companions received the Macedonian vision that led them into continental Europe, a decision which set the destiny for modern Christianity.

This seems simple, but there must have been an agonizing search for the right strategy throughout this experience.

In one way or another, Paul was seeking God's blueprint for missions in the first century world. It is hardly accidental that he would spend his energies establishing "mission base" churches in the metropolitan centers: Philippi, Corinth, Thessalonica and Ephesus.

Acts depicts the broad strokes of the *arketekton*. But careful inspection also reveals exacting details. In each city, Paul quickly followed his adopted pattern, seeking those who were spiritually sensitive to revealed truth through the Scriptures. He would enter the synagogue and speak first to the Jews. But his greatest response was from the "God-fearers," those Gentiles who had adopted the God of Abraham, Isaac and Jacob, but who had not submitted to circumcision. These became his nuclei for reaching the multitudes of the Gentile world through the successful multiplication of Gentile Christian churches. This was his plan of action for churching the Roman world.

Planning in the early church

Paul was not the first to employ strategies for growth and expansion. Acts 6:1-7 gives a remarkable insight into the planning employed by the church soon after Pentecost. This account of choosing " the seven" lay leaders in the Jerusalem church, begins and closes with two strong statements of growth. Acts 6:1 states, "And in those days when the number of disciples was multiplied. . ." Acts 6:7 closes with the statement, "The number of disciples multiplied in Jerusalem greatly."

The intervening verses found in Acts 6:2-6 strongly imply that growth for the Jerusalem church had reached a plateau. Some imbalance in the evangelistic outreach and internal ministry was hindering the multiplication of disciples. In one of the most dramatic moments in Scripture, the

Jesus was teaching the importance of wise planning. The goal of his strategy, discipling of the nations, will continue to elude the church until it employs adequate planning.

75

church paused to seek the solution to this dilemma so that once again the number of disciples might be multiplied.

The manner in which these early disciples handled the problem is instructive to the 20th century church. In very clear fashion they modeled methods for problem solving which resulted in continuing multiplication growth.

Gathering information

Aware of a blockage preventing the multiplication of disciples, the church first gathered information to identify the cause. How this was done in the Jerusalem church is not clear. But their focus was: the Greek-speaking widows were being neglected in the daily ministry. This accurate diagnosis was the the first essential step toward developing strategy for multiplying disciples.

Yet often this is neglected. Instead, churches with declining or plateaued membership line up at the patent medicine counters of programs and projects.

Considering alternatives

Once the diagnosis was made, church leaders considered remedial action. This is indicated by the statement, "It is not right that we should leave the Word of God and serve tables." This public statement reflected the leaders' consideration of at least two possible actions. Some may have suggested rearranging schedules to provide more time for ministry to the Greek-speaking widows. Others responded that this would also occupy the creative leadership needed for prayer and preaching of the Word.

Additional alternatives may have been considered, but the leaders had considered at least two and rejected one.

Too often the church is not selective in its approach to dealing with problems. Like a man who treats his cold with a variety of medicines then feels worse after the medications interact with the others, many churches respond to temporary problems with "overkill."

All alternatives should be considered. But not every proposal to help the immediate problem will necessarily produce desired results.

The Jerusalem church saw neglected widows as the problem. But its immediate solution did not ensure a cure for the church. The church needed a way to care for the widows and nurture continued growth.

All alternatives should be considered. But not every proposal to help the immediate problem will necessarily produce desired results.

Involving the whole church

The third step involves the entire church in the solution. "Wherefore brethren, look ye out among you seven men." The disciples could have easily taken this task into their own hands had they distrusted the people of God. How easily verse three could have read: "Wherefore brethren, we have selected seven men." Healthy solutions to disciple multiplication must include God's people. The church must learn to trust and depend upon the laity.

The fourth step in effective planning is implementation. Many good strategies gather dust from neglect. Churches have often rallied to adoption of well designed projects only to have their dreams fade, phantomlike, through the veil of procrastination. Unless dreams become reality, unless strategies are implemented, the entire process remains futile.

The Jerusalem church implemented its strategy. The apostles practiced delegation of authority and ministry while the people accepted the care extended by chosen lay leaders. These seven began their *diakoneo*, their service to the Greek-speaking widows.

The final stage of the process is evaluation. "The Word of God increased, and the number of disciples multiplied in Jerusalem greatly; and a great company of the priests were obedient to the faith." Their plan worked well; the desired results were accomplished. Otherwise, the entire process would have begun again.

Here is an element often missed in the current approach to expansion strategy. While churches seldom gather enough information to analyze alternatives, and fewer implement what is designed, only rarely do they pause to evaluate. Adopted programs and strategies continue intact without consideration for their effectiveness.

Without the evaluation, initial problems may continue unsolved or be compounded by partial cures. Programming without evaluation can easily focus the great powers of the church on side issues and fall short of the "one thing that is needful."

Bold planning must be rediscovered if the church is to carry out Jesus Christ's Great Commission. This is the key which unlocks the door to catalytic missions, the essential

> *Many good strategies gather dust from neglect. Churches have often rallied to adoption of well designed projects only to have their dreams fade.*

ingredient which produces a chain reaction of multiplied churches and disciples. Certainly some missions will be accomplished without planning. Some churches will be born. But these usually will occur out of colonizing—or a response mode—when denominations respond to isolated groups who request a church.

A few missions will develop around a catalytic individual who starts the work on his own initiative. Others will develop from the natural splits which take place within congregations. But the number of these churches will be relatively small. Seldom will inroads be made beyond the dominant cultural and language group in which the denomination has its roots. Lutherans will continue to start churches in pockets of German and Scandinavian people. Episcopalians will continue to respond to requests of upper-middle and upper-class Anglos who desire the liturgical expressions of their parents. Methodists and Presbyterians will continue to church the increasingly professional and wealthy Anglo populace. Southern Baptists will continue to form churches for transplanted Southerners who speak with a drawl and who long for a church like the one of their youth.

Penetration of the population will dwindle as unchurched minorities outstrip the immigration and birthrates of European Americans. Generational dropouts will increase among the previously churched. Secularism will continue to spread as the biological growth of the church falters behind that of the world.

A spiritually illiterate generation will replace that of its devout forebears.

Only by adopting the planning process of Paul and the Jerusalem Apostles will the church regain the offensive and aggressively attack the fortress of darkness.

One of the best examples of this process is the ministry of Enrique Torres, Hispanic director of the Los Angeles American Baptists. Torres, a native of Chile, is an immigrant to America. Currently he directs the missions strategy of American Baptists in Los Angeles, California, a city with a concentration of Hispanics second only to Mexico City.

Amid this rapidly growing population, he is effectively initiating one American Baptist church per month with no financial capital. His resource is planning: (1) isolate a

*B*old planning must be rediscovered if the church is to carry out Jesus Christ's Great Commission. This is the key which unlocks the door to catalytic missions.

78

geographic target area; (2) develop a feasibility study detailing the demographics of that area: ethnicity, income, educational level, population trends, existing churches; (3) enlist a sponsor church; (4) develop a mission strategy; (5) enlist a mission pastor; (6) launch the mission.

This approach is resulting in a turnaround for American Baptists in Los Angeles. Anglo congregations that were dying in Hispanic areas are giving birth to new, vibrant, Hispanic churches. It is not unusual for the Hispanic congregation meeting in the facilities of the Anglo church to outnumber its mother congregation in little more than a year.

This approach reflects the catalytic mode of the New Testament rather than the colonizing approach of more recent mission work.

The writing of Acts did not give rise to catalytic dimensions expressed in the pages of that book. Rather, the experience of the catalytic missions prompted Luke's account.

Those who lift up their eyes to the fields, analyze the nature of the harvest, design appropriate strategies, then enter the harvest with indefatigable commitment will find themselves participating in church growth as documented on the pages of the New Testament.

Questions for pastors and churches:

1. Has growth stopped in our congregation?

2. What are the possible blockages to continued growth in our church?

3. What are some alternative solutions to the blockages to growth in our church?

4. What is the best solution?

5. How can we involve the people of the church in the process of identifying and solving impediments to growth?

6. Has our church implemented its proposals of the past?

7. Are there some programs in our church that need re-evaluation?

8. Are sections of our population not being reached by our church or denomination?

9. How can our church conduct "catalytic" missions that will penetrate population groups currently not being reached?

THE

Gro

DIMENSION

Barriers to growth exist within certain ranges of average attendance. These barriers are as real—and as invisible—as gravity and inertia. To deal with these barriers the church may use a series of growth principles which relate to sociological factors of grouping, ministering and relationships.

The core group

The first range of resistance to church growth will occur within the "core group" (see Table 4). This range is encountered when a church averages 30-40 in attendance.

Usually a new church will grow rapidly to an attendance of 30, a "random" grouping of previously unrelated people drawn together by mutual interest in forming a congregation. These members will experience a need to relate to one another more meaningfully. With time, they will build trust by sharing needs, weaknesses, strengths, vision and faith.

Eventually this group begins to see itself as a church where spiritual and emotional hungers are satisfied. Sharing is intimate and informal. Everyone is known by name, including the children. Special events, such as birthdays, anniversaries, births and graduations are a "congregational" experience. This personal bonding is an essential base for the church. Without it, families will become disillusioned and discouraged. Their spiritual lives will wither, and one by one they will move out of the congregation. Without bonding, the effort will fail.

Church growth moves easily from an average attendance of 30 to 50. After that, however, the dynamics change. It is difficult to maintain close relationships with all the members.

Dissolution of the core group is an emotional adjustment. The pastor's coffee visits and phone calls become less frequent. The informal Bible study led by the pastor who relates to members like a "buddy" becomes more formal. Close friendships within the core are diffused as energy is focused on new families. Because members are unwilling to sacrifice either the informality of a close-knit core or regular contact with the pastor, few churches grow beyond this range. Even though names and faces change, and even though many churches reach 60 to 80 in attendance, eventually most return to the core number.

A church may break the core group only as it chooses to pay the price of developing a broad-based organization. Once this happens, the church may experience rapid and virtually unhindered growth until it enters the next range.

Church growth moves easily from an average attendance of 30 to 50. After that the dynamics change. It is difficult to maintain close relationships with all the members.

The congregational range

The congregational range exists at an average attendance of 100, plus or minus 20. It is characterized by organizational expansion with multiple "core" groups. Sunday School is probably the key program for accomplishing this.

Whereas the "core group" works well with one adult department composed of two or three classes, the "congregational" stage requires at least two adult departments with two to five adult classes in each. With two or more "core groups" built around these departments, the church at least doubles its assimilation potential.

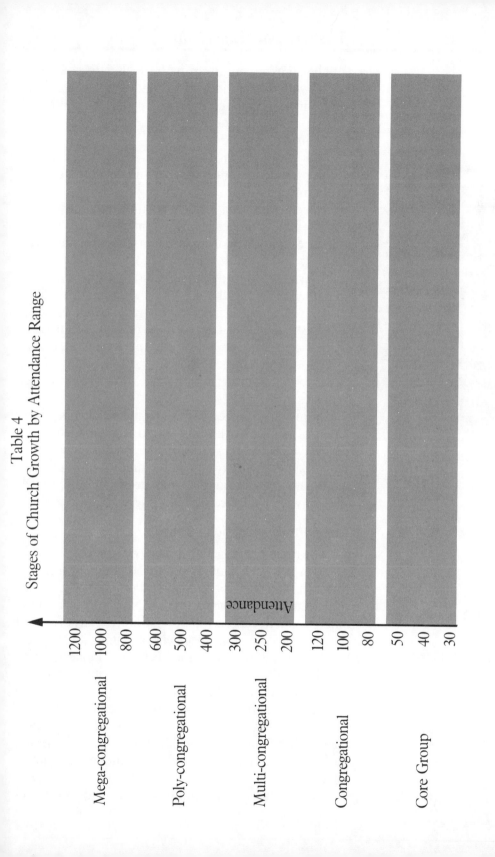

Table 4
Stages of Church Growth by Attendance Range

The closeknit core group may resist the larger organization. It will separate individuals and couples who have bonded in the original core group. But the longer a church remains in the core group stage, the less likely a congregation will move beyond it.

New churches have attempted a variety of ways to group people, including shared life-concerns or age. Southern Baptist efforts to group people for Bible study and evangelism by age can scarcely be improved upon. Even various ethnic churches are discovering the universal principles of Sunday School organization. An enrollment ceiling of 25 for an adult Sunday School class maintains a healthy small group dynamic. This dynamic is further strengthened within the class by the assignments for a teacher, outreach leader and group leaders responsible for no more than five persons, each. As enrollment surpasses 25, new classes are organized and this facilitates growth.

An adult department may consist of as many as five classes. After that, creation of a new department further facilitates growth.

In this range, space becomes a matter of concern. A variety of inexpensive facilities would accommodate a core group of 40; however, a church in the congregational range needs a larger, better equipped building. While buildings and organization do not guarantee growth, church development will be affected by both.

The multi-congregational range

The multi-congregational range occurs when average attendance is 250, plus or minus 50. Prior to this, the church has operated as one congregation, with perhaps two adult Sunday School departments. Now the nuclei of the different congregations will develop around any of several centers: music, youth, evangelism training, day ministries—or length of church membership. "Pioneers" who established the church may emerge as distinct from the more recently arrived "homesteaders." In fact, the development of healthy interest groups is essential to growth.

These distinct congregations, whatever their center, may easily be interpreted as cliques which could threaten the harmony and unity of the church. But this need not be the case.

These distinct congregations, whatever their center, may easily be interpreted as cliques which could threaten the harmony and unity of the church. But this need not be the case.

Movement into the multi-congregational range requires a new style of pastoral leadership which majors on delegation. Responsibilities previously handled by the pastor must be delegated to paid staff or volunteer laypersons.

At this point, the pastor faces a dilemma similar to that mentioned in Acts 6. In the context of Christ's teachings on servanthood, the apostles may have felt a certain compulsion to wait on tables. At the same time, the Greek-speaking widows probably enjoyed their attention. But continued growth of the Jerusalem church required delegation. Consequently, the apostles enlisted the congregation to select seven men to perform this ministry to the widows. This released the apostles to spend time in prayer and ministry of the word.

As a congregation peers across the border of growth into the multi-congregational dimension, decisions must be made by pastor and people. The pastor must be willing to trust others with tasks he has previously performed. He may no longer be able to visit every person who enters the hospital or sit with families in the waiting room, soothe every ruffled feather, conduct every committee meeting or monitor every expenditure.

If the pastor cannot determine priorities, church growth will be limited by his capacity to meet its needs. His frustration level will increase exponentially to its growth. And satisfaction of the members will diminish proportionately.

The decision to delegate must be shared by the congregation. Critical to the proposal of Acts 6 was its acceptance by the people: "And the statement found approval with the whole congregation" (Acts 6:5, NASB).

Members of the church must be willing to accept the ministry of a deacon who "waits upon their table." The congregation must accept delegated ministry, in order for the church to become multi-congregational.

All the skills of able leadership, Christian compassion, understanding and diplomacy are necessary to lead the church successfully through turbulent waters that open into the congregational stage. Most churches are unable to chart this difficult course.

The poly-congregational range

The poly-congregational barrier occurs at 500 average attendance, plus or minus 100.

While double and triple worship services and dual Sunday Schools may reach the multi-congregational church, growth into the poly-congregational stage will probably mean the church needs to add space, often entailing hundreds of thousands of dollars.

Among options to expensive building projects are satellite churches. Through these congregations, meeting in storefront buildings, clubrooms, apartments and homes, one church can reach various social, economic and cultural groups with minimal expense.

In this range, pressures for clerical and professional staff intensify with congregational demands for specialized ministries. Yet much can be accomplished through involvement of the laity. Without high level lay involvement, the church runs the risk of housing members who are ministered to rather than becoming ministers. Wise decisions in staffing can enhance the discipling and ministering of the church in the poly-congregational stage.

The mega-congregational range

The mega-congregational barrier exists at 1,000 average attendance, plus or minus 200. This stage requires further adjustment on the part of the pastor. At this range of growth, the pastor must become primarily administrator and preacher. He is further removed from the daily life of members at large; an expanded staff requires his expertise in areas of recruitment, delegation, supervision and review.

The pastor of the mega-congregation may spend as much time supervising and coordinating his staff as the pastor of the core-group church spends pastoring his people. Added to this administrative load is management of a complex budget which in the case of many churches may amount to $1 million or more, annually.

As the pastor has less personal contact with members, the preaching event becomes increasingly important. Effective public speaking which communicates sensitivity to daily concerns and understanding of the Scriptures, is essential.

Unique congregations that break the mega-congregational barrier with an attendance of 2,000 to 5,000, must have uniquely gifted pastors, men with spiritual charismata and social charisma.

The church must be willing to accept the ministry of a deacon who "waits upon their table," delegated ministry, in order for the church to become multi-congregational.

86

Few churches reach the poly- or mega-congregational range. But a church of 100 that gives birth to many new churches will eventually reach more people than a mega-congregational church which starts no new congregations.

The multiplication of churches provides a logical means for affecting the non-Christian world.

Consider the pecan farmer. He may try to coax a greater harvest by investing his time and energy on a few large pecan trees, or he may plant a number of new trees. At first, the yield from the new trees will not be as high as that from a single large tree. But in time, the young trees will multiply the harvest.

The planting of many new churches will result in a multiplied harvest.

Questions for pastors and churches:

1. Into what range does our church fall?

2. What are the obstacles that hinder our church from further growth?

3. What are the principles affecting our church in its present growth range?

4. What actions must our church take to encourage growth into the next range?

5. Does our church want to grow beyond its current range? What do we consider to be optimum size for our congregation?

6. If our church reached its optimum growth, how many people would still remain unreached in our community?

7. Could our church multiply its outreach by giving birth to other congregations?

About the Author

In 1976, with fewer than 10 members, William Tinsley started First Baptist Church, The Colony, Texas. In seven years, Sunday School enrollment had grown to 900, and under Tinsley's guidance, this young church had successfully started two other congregations: Colony Park Baptist Church and Friendship Baptist Church.

Since 1982, Tinsley has helped coordinate church starting statewide through the Baptist General Convention of Texas.

He is a graduate of Baylor University and has a Doctor of Ministry degree from Southwestern Baptist Theological Seminary in Fort Worth, Texas.

He and his wife, Jacqueline, have three children.